An Hachette UK Company
www.hachette.co.uk

First published in the United Kingdom in 2022
by Ilex, an imprint of
Octopus Publishing Group Ltd
Carmelite House
50 Victoria Embankment
London EC4Y 0DZ
www.octopusbooks.co.uk
www.octopusbooksusa.com

Distributed in the US by Hachette Book Group
1290 Avenue of the Americas, 4th & 5th Floors,
New York, NY 101014

Distributed in Canada by Canadian Manda Group
664 Annette Street, Toronto, Ontario,
Canada M6S 2C8

Design and layout copyright
© Octopus Publishing Group Ltd 2022
Text copyright © Juliet Uzor 2022

Publisher: Alison Starling
Commissioning Editor: Ellie Corbett
Managing Editor: Rachel Silverlight
Assistant Editor: Ellen Sandford O'Neill
Art Director: Ben Gardiner
Design: Studio Polka
Layout: Tammy Kerr
Photographer: Kim Lightbody
Illustrator: Caitlin Keegan
Stylist: Rachel Vere
Pattern Cutting and Grading: Grade House
Pattern Review: Christina Walsh
Production Manager: Caroline Alberti

ISBN 978-1-78157-822-3

A CIP catalogue record for this book is available
from the British Library.

Printed and bound in China

10 9 8 7 6 5 4 3 2

YOU WILL BE ABLE TO SEW YOUR OWN CLOTHES BY THE END OF THIS BOOK

JULIET UZOR

ilex

Introduction

Projects

Upcycling

ESSENTIAL SKILLS

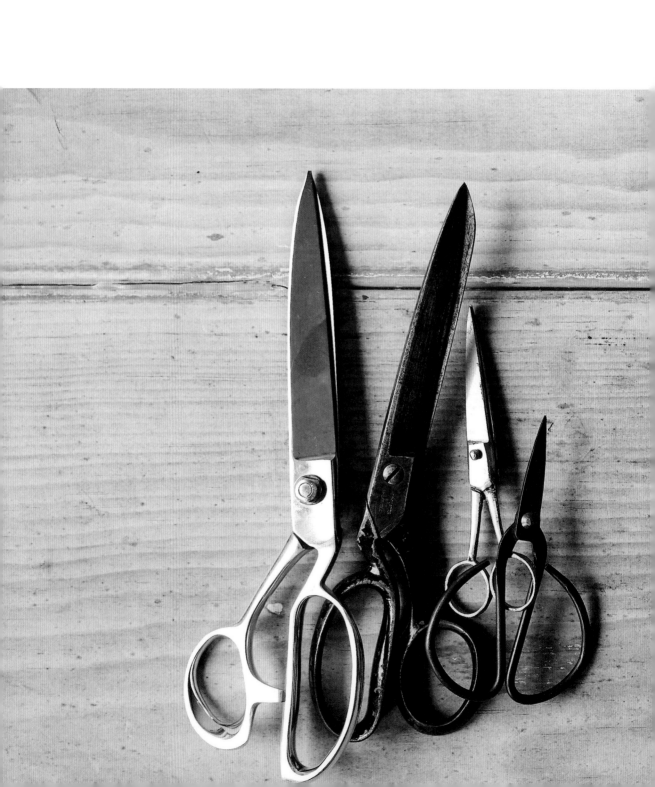

Introduction

Learning to sew

Deciding to learn how to sew, and being able to clothe myself in whatever garment or fabric type I choose and tailor it to my changing body, has been one of the most liberating decisions of my adult life. The same can be true for you, too!

From the outside, with all the complicated-looking gadgets and apparently unattainable techniques, sewing can seem very intimidating – but once you have the basics down, it's much easier than you might think.

As someone who didn't learn to operate a sewing machine until the age of 29, I've been careful to cut out the fluff in this introduction to sewing and get straight into sharing the important skills that enabled me to sew clothes from day one.

Once you've picked up some basic knowledge about choosing fabric, taking measurements, using a pattern and everyday sewing skills, I suggest it's best to jump straight into your first project. There are 15 in the book, ranging from a simple headband to an elegant wrap dress and ideas for upcycling existing garments. As you work through them you'll come across new techniques, such as inserting zips, neckline facings and bias binding, that you can use in projects of your own. So whether you are interested in learning a new craft or are simply fed up of being at the mercy of clothing stores, you will, by the end of this book, get to the point of being able to say, 'I made it myself!'

Juliet Uzor
@julietuzor_

Basic sewing kit

Although there are countless sewing gizmos and gadgets on the market, the good news is that very few of them are absolutely essential. Here are my suggestions for a basic sewing kit; if other more specialized tools are needed for a particular project, I've mentioned them as an extra.

THE ESSENTIALS

Sewing machine

Sewing machine feet: All-purpose, zip and buttonhole

Sewing machine needles: Universal needles, jersey needles and denim needles

Bobbins

Pins

Hand sewing needles

Flexible measuring tape

Ruler

Sewing gauge

Tailor's chalk

Water-soluble or heat-erasable pen

Dressmaker's carbon paper and tracing wheel

Dressmaker's shears and/or rotary cutter and self-healing cutting mat

Thread snips

Stitch ripper

Pinking shears

Iron and ironing board

Pressing cloth

Tailor's ham

Washi or masking tape

Chopstick or knitting needle

SEWING TOOLS

The first thing you need to sew your own clothes is a sewing machine. Why a sewing machine instead of a needle? The simple answer is that if you want to create robust, wearable garments, machine stitching is the best way to achieve this. The stitches are more consistent, professional looking and faster to sew.

Your first sewing machine need not be very expensive; in fact, at the start of your sewing journey, it's worth considering borrowing or renting one. For simple projects, including those in this book, all you really need are the straight and zig-zag stitching functions, although a buttonhole function is an added bonus. A simple, inexpensive sewing machine should still come with all the most important attachments – an all-purpose foot, a zip foot, a buttonhole foot, spare bobbins and a basic machine maintenance kit.

To complete the projects in this book, you will need a few different kinds of sewing machine needle, as listed in the table opposite. It's important to match the needle size to the weight of fabric you're using: as a general rule, the more lightweight the fabric, the thinner the needle you will use. It's a good idea to invest in some spare bobbins, so that you can keep them wound with the colours you use most regularly.

With the basics covered, you can move on to familiarizing yourself with your machine works. All sewing machines are built differently, so read your sewing machine manual thoroughly in order to understand what the parts are and how they function. Practise threading your bobbin and sewing machine, raising and lowering the presser foot and sewing in straight lines over and over again on pieces of old, scrap or recycled fabrics. This will help you to gain control of your machine, maintain consistent rows of stitches and learn the functions of the various buttons.

In addition to a sewing machine, you will also need pins, which you will use to pin pattern pieces to your fabric and to hold pieces of fabric together before you sew them. You will find pins with both plastic and glass heads. Coloured pin heads are easier to see against the fabric (and when you drop them!); glass heads have the advantage of not melting if you accidentally iron over them. It's also worth having a few hand-sewing needles in your kit for temporary stitches, for certain finishes and for sewing on buttons and snap fasteners.

MEASURING TOOLS

To achieve accurate results in the clothes you make, the most
important piece of advice is to measure many times and cut once.
I recommend that you have the following three measuring tools
in your arsenal: a flexible measuring tape for measuring yourself;
a ruler for accurate measurements and for drawing straight lines;
and a sewing gauge for marking seams, hems and smaller parts of
garments such as collars, facings and cuffs.

MARKING TOOLS

These tools are used for transferring marks from sewing patterns
to your fabric (see page 33) and for tracing templates onto fabrics.
There is a wide range of mark-making tools on the market, from
traditional tailor's chalk to water-soluble pens, heat-erasable pens
and dressmaker's carbon paper and a tracing wheel. You may need
different tools based on the fabric you are using, and it is worth first
testing them out on a scrap piece of your chosen fabric to make sure
they behave as you want them to.

CUTTING TOOLS

Dressmaker's shears or a rotary cutter are ideal for cutting out most
fabrics. Bear in mind that you should keep a separate set of scissors
just for cutting fabric and avoid using them for anything else such as
paper or card. If you opt for a rotary cutter, then you will also need a
self-healing cutting mat. Dressmaker's shears have an angled handle
that allows you to cut without having to lift the fabric up from the
table, reducing the risk of the fabric sliding around and causing
inaccurate cutting. They come in different lengths – 20–23cm
(8–9in) is a good length to start with, as it allows you to make fairly
long, smooth cuts yet still cut tight corners. If you are doing a lot of
sewing, you should have your shears professionally sharpened on a
regular basis.

Other important cutting tools include thread snips for cutting off stray threads while sewing, stitch rippers (also known as seam rippers or unpickers) for undoing any mistakes, and pinking shears for giving the raw edges of fabrics a clean, zig-zag finish to reduce the possibility of fraying.

FINISHING TOOLS

An iron is essential, as you should press the fabric at every stage of the sewing process to 'set' the stitches and create neat seams. Do ensure that your iron is of good quality, with a steam option and a range of heat settings. You will also require a pressing cloth to prevent making iron marks on fragile fabrics and to protect your fabrics from scorching. Always remember to test the heat setting of your iron first on a scrap piece of your project fabric.

An ironing board (tabletop or full-sized) is essential, and a tailor's ham is a useful addition for pressing the curved parts of a garment.

USEFUL EXTRAS

These may not sound like obvious tools for making your own clothes, but a small strip of washi or masking tape applied to the throat plate of your machine 1.5cm (⅝in) from the needle will make it easier to keep your seam allowances a consistent width – just keep the edge of your fabric lined up with the edge of the tape as you sew. And a chopstick or knitting needle is extremely useful for pushing corners out to a neat point when you turn items right side out.

INTRODUCTION

Fabrics

The freedom to wear clothes in fabrics of any colour, design, pattern, texture or heritage is one of the greatest advantages of learning to sew your own clothes. Through these textiles, we can explore the artistic aspect of sewing – but there are elements to consider beyond that. The first things to consider are the way the fabric is constructed and whether it's made from natural or manmade fibres.

WOVEN OR KNIT?

Woven fabrics

Any fabric that has its fibres horizontally and vertically interwoven is a woven fabric. Woven fabrics include cotton (arguably the biggest sewing staple when it comes to fabric), drill, chiffon, polyester, silk, denim, corduroy, crepe, georgette, velvet and many more. Woven fabrics are mostly created without stretch properties, except those blended with other types of fibre or when they are cut on the bias, at a 45-degree angle (see page 31).

Woven fabric comes in a wide variety of colours, patterns and fibre types, including natural and synthetic fibres. It is worth noting that woven fabrics may be stiff (upholstery fabrics) or lightweight (georgette fabrics), but they share a basic fact in common: irrelevant of their composition, their edges will fray when cut. The level of fraying differs from fabric to fabric.

Woven fabrics are a good choice for beginners because they are much more stable, easy to control and hardly stretch out of shape as you work with them.

Knit fabrics

These fabrics have their fibres looped together to form either two-way stretch fabrics or four-way stretch fabrics. Two-way stretch fabrics stretch in only two directions, while four-way stretch fabrics can stretch left, right, up and down. Jersey, which is mostly used for T-shirts, is an example of a knit fabric. There are also athletic and dance fabrics that are made from spandex, another type of knit fabric.

Knit fabrics need to be handled and sewn in a slightly different way to woven fabrics – see page 69.

NATURAL OR MANMADE?

Fabrics can be made up of either natural or manmade fibres. Natural fibres come from plants such as cotton, bamboo, flax and so on, or are animal-based, like wool and silk (which comes from silkworms). Manmade fibres include polyester, nylon and spandex. These fibres are twisted and made into yarns that are then either knitted or woven into fabrics. Fabrics made from natural fibres tend to be more breathable, making them more comfortable to wear in the summer months, but they can lose their shape with washing. Manmade fabrics are hard-wearing and retain their shape well, and they are often easier to wash and care for, but they are not as gentle on the skin.

Most man-made fibres are made with processes using crude oil, and unlike natural fibres, they are not biodegradable, so in general, natural fabrics are a more environmentally friendly option. However, it's worth remembering that natural fibres are derived from plants and animals that require space and water to grow or rear them, as well as people to process them, and not all natural fabrics are equally sustainable. Searching for ethical and sustainable suppliers and researching different fabrics will help you make informed choices.

SELECTING THE RIGHT FABRIC

It is easy to feel overwhelmed when buying fabric because of the way fabrics are organized in stores and online. Some fabric stores organize their wares based on their purpose – for example, fashion fabrics, special occasion fabrics, quilting, upholstery etc. – and this makes the selection process slightly tricky.

Fabrics come in bolts of differing widths (commonly 112cm/45in and 150cm/60in). You may well be tempted to immediately buy all the fabrics your heart desires, but it is important to pay close attention to the recommendations that accompany sewing patterns. This is because different fabrics behave in different ways, so will only be suitable for certain projects. The sewing projects in this book come with lists of suggested fabrics for optimum results, as do commercial sewing patterns, so it is worth deciding which project you are going to make before purchasing your fabric. Check your garment pattern instructions beforehand to ensure that you purchase the right amount of fabric and the width specified. Bear in mind that if you want to pattern match, you may need more fabric than the pattern calls for.

It's also important to feel the fabric; even if you're buying online, most suppliers will let you order a small sample swatch. Think about the weight of the fabric and whether that's appropriate for the type of garment you're making: do you want a light, floaty fabric for a blouse or something more heavy duty, such as denim, for a skirt? Does it crease easily, like linen? Can you wash it or does it need to be dry cleaned?

COMMON FABRIC TYPES

Cotton

A natural fibre, cotton is known for its versatility, with many
different weaves, weights and blends available. Cotton fabrics do
not slip or slide like their light-weight counterparts, but are sturdy,
stable and easy to cut, sew and iron, making them very popular
with beginner sewers. Cotton fabrics should be machine washed
at 30/40°C before use and steam pressed on a hot setting.

Denim

Denim is a sturdy, cotton-based fabric that is available in different
weights and is sometimes combined with elastic fibres for some
stretch. Heavier-weight denim fabrics are best sewn using purpose-
made heavy-duty sewing needles, which should be size 14/16.
Denim should be washed separately at 30/40°C before use and
steam pressed on a hot setting.

Jersey

Jersey is another cotton-based fabric that is known for its softness and
elasticity. It comes in a range of blends, weights, weaves and stretch
capacities, including French terry, Ponte Roma, double knit, interlock
and sweater knit. Jersey fabrics drape very well and should be sewn
using ballpoint needles (size 11/12) because the knitted nature of their
fibres. Jersey fabrics shrink a lot so pre-washing is advised at 30°C.
For more information on working with knit fabrics, see page 69.

Linen

Made from flax, linen is one of the most sustainable fabrics available,
but it is well known for its tendency to crease. Linen fabric works
well with dresses, shirts, trousers, skirts and lightweight summer-
style jackets. Since it is prone to fraying, it is better to finish the raw
edges using zig-zag stitches or overlocking before manipulating the
fabric pieces. Do not finish the raw edges with pinking shears; due
to the weave, it will fray before you have finished constructing your
piece. Linen should be machine washed at 30/40°C before use and
steam pressed on a hot setting.

<u>Viscose</u>

Also known as rayon, viscose is manmade fabric that is easy to work with and popular among home sewers. Viscose fabrics are suitable for dresses, blouses and lightweight outerwear garments. They tend to fray more than cotton fabrics and should be finished using zig-zag stitches, overlocking or using pinking shears. Viscose fabrics should be machine washed before use at 30°C and steam pressed on a low heat setting.

CARING FOR FABRIC BEFORE SEWING

There are many 'low-maintenance' fabrics that require little to no special treatment but others, such as delicate silks, georgettes and some brocades, have fibres that can easily become snagged by a slightly rough surface or have their raw edges begin to fray and shred even without contact with any surfaces. In some cases, it is advised to 'finish' the raw cut edges of these types of fabrics before you store or even wash them. This can be done using an overlocker or zig-zag stitches on your sewing machine (see page 40).

It is also very important to wash your fabric before you use it for any sewing project. This ensures that any shrinkage occurs before you start to sew, rather than after you've made your garment. It also removes any extra dye from the fabric. Note, however, that not all fabrics can be washed before a sewing with them, including wools and silks, especially dupion, which will permanently crease.

Take some time to look out for the specific care instructions for a fabric on the bolt at the store when you buy it. Take a photograph or jot them down on your receipt. Fabric store staff are usually happy to share fabric care guidelines with their customers. Care instructions and fibre content are generally shared on the websites of online fabric retailers, so read the fine print before ordering and make a note of the details.

Taking measurements

A common mistake among beginners to sewing is to select their sewing pattern size based on their standard shop-bought clothes size. If you want to make clothes that fit perfectly, you need to take your own measurements.

To measure yourself as accurately as possible, you need to wear close-fitting clothes. It's also a good idea to wear the undergarments that you would wear with the garment you're making.

To determine your true/natural waist location, tie a length of thin elastic around your waist and move around a little. The elastic will settle around your true waist. You will then be able to measure yourself with a tape measure or ask a friend to help you. Remember to stand as straight as possible, look forward and allow the measuring tape to be as horizontal or as straight as possible.

The key measurements that you will need to create the garments in this book are:

Bust: Ensure the measuring tape is firmly around the fullest part of your bust.

Waist: This measurement should be made around the thin elastic you tied around your true waist.

Hip: This is the measurement around the widest part of your bottom, commonly between the waist and the top of your legs.

Pattern sizing

The patterns in this book are based on a woman 165cm (5ft 4in) tall and are graded to 10 different sizes. Use this measurement chart as a guideline to determine where to cut out your sewing pattern. From there, you can make all the adjustments you need in order to get the perfect fit.

SIZE	BUST cm/in	WAIST cm/in	HIP cm/in
6	79cm | 31in	64cm | 25in	89cm | 35in
8	84cm | 33in	66cm | 26in	92cm | 36in
10	86cm | 34in	69cm | 27in	94cm | 37in
12	92cm | 36in	71cm | 28in	97cm | 38in
14	97cm | 38in	76cm | 30in	102cm | 40in
16	102cm | 40in	81cm | 32in	107cm | 42in
18	107cm | 42in	89cm | 35in	112cm | 44in
20	112cm | 44in	97cm | 38in	117cm | 46in
22	117cm | 46in	102cm | 40in	122cm | 48in
24	122cm | 48in	107cm | 42in	127cm | 50n
26	127cm | 50in	112cm | 44in	132cm | 52in
28	132cm | 52in	117cm | 46in	137cm | 54in

Blending pattern sizes

BLENDING PATTERN SIZES

When selecting your size from the chart opposite, you may find that some of your body measurements might not fully match the sizes in the chart. If your measurements appear across multiple sizes, you will need to blend the pattern sizes to get your true size.

This means that a person with, say, a bust of 102cm (40in), a waist of 97cm (38in) and hips of 117cm (46in) can still sew a garment for themselves by combining sizes 16 and 20. This is done by drawing a smooth line to join the size 16 line needed for the bust with the size 20 line of the waist and hips. The armhole, neckline and sleeves will not be affected. After you've made adjustments to the front pattern piece, remember to make the same adjustment on the back piece too, to keep things balanced.

TESTING SEWING PATTERNS FOR FIT

Just like the clothes you might try on in a store, sewing patterns probably won't fit perfectly every time. Pattern houses use standard 'fit models' on which they base their sewing patterns, but your body is unique; you will need to test any new pattern before you use it to create your final garment. Factor in some inexpensive fabric or old soft furnishings and some time to make a 'mock-up' garment, known as a toile or a muslin. You should do this any time you have made changes to a sewing pattern or are stitching it up for the first time. It might seem like a laborious process, but the end results are absolutely worth the effort – in the long run, it saves time, energy and your precious fabric.

The simplest way to test a pattern is to cut the fabric to the size above what you think you should be, then it should only ever need to be taken in, by pinching, pleating and pinning the excess fabric along the seams or darts, and then transferring the adjustments to the pattern pieces. If, on the other hand, the toile is too small, you will find that the fabric pulls in whichever area requires adjusting. To remedy this, you will need to make adjustments to allow for more fabric in those places – for example, by opening out side seams or shoulder seams or loosening darts. Then transfer any adjustments to your sewing pattern.

Tip:
It's best to try on a toile with the wrong side of the fabric facing out, so that you can make transfer any adjustments easily.

Adjusting sewing patterns

By taking the time to test out a new pattern on a toile, you will have the opportunity to adjust the pattern before you make the real thing. A few simple adjustments can make all the difference to achieving a perfect fit.

There are a range of adjustments that can be made to sewing patterns to ensure that they fit your unique body type, shape and size. Bust adjustments, narrow or wide shoulder adjustments, hip adjustment, waist adjustment, back adjustment, shortening and lengthening pieces... the list is endless. One of the simplest ways to customize a pattern is to shorten or lengthen the pieces as you like.

In order to make a simple length adjustment to a sewing pattern, you will need to work perpendicular to the grain line of the fabric. To shorten a sewing pattern, draw a straight line across the pattern piece, avoiding the darts and any important markings, then another line parallel to the first at the distance equal to the amount you wish to shorten the pattern piece by. Fold one line to the other and use some sticky tape to hold the crease in place. To lengthen a pattern piece, draw a straight line across the piece and cut along it, then stick the two pieces to a new sheet of paper at a distance equal to the amount you wish to lengthen your pattern by, and redraw the outer lines of the pattern.

BUST ADJUSTMENTS

Altering the bust is one of the most common adjustments you will need to make to a pattern, and you will notice the difference it makes when you achieve a perfectly fitting garment.

If there are wrinkles above or below the bust on your toile, then that's a clear indication that a bust adjustment is required. To make any adjustments here, you will need some extra paper, sticky tape, a pair of scissors and a pattern ruler (or any other ruler with markings for checking for right angles).

Tip:
Remember to make length adjustments equally to any corresponding pattern pieces (e.g. front and back pattern pieces) and smoothen any broken lines with a ruler and pencil.

Lowering the bust point

If wrinkles appear above the bust on your toile, then you need to lower the bust point on your pattern piece.

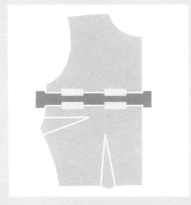

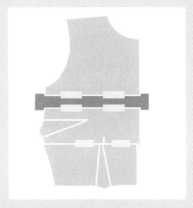

Step 1: Draw a horizontal line across the bust point, ensuring that it is horizontal to the centre front line.

Step 2: Cut along this line and separate the pattern pieces by the amount required. Stick the pieces to a new sheet of paper and redraw the centre front and side edges.

Tip:
Note that the original grain line of the sewing pattern must remain straight to ensure that the final garment is cut correctly.

Step 3: Remember to shorten the bodice to its original length by shortening it just above the waistline. To do this, draw two parallel lines that are exactly the same width apart as the amount by which you lengthened the bodice to lower the bust.

Raising the bust point

If wrinkles appear below the bust on your toile, then you need to raise the bust point on your pattern piece.

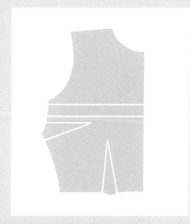 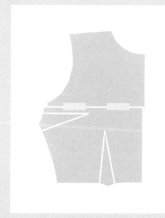 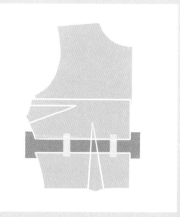

Step 1: Draw two parallel lines across the bodice sewing pattern piece just below the bust point. These lines must be at right angles to the centre front of your pattern and should be the same distance apart as the amount by which the bust point should be raised.

Step 2: Carefully fold the pattern along the bottom line and line up the folded edge with the top line. Stick these two surfaces together to raise the bust line. At this point, the side front and centre front edges will look jagged. Simply redraw them by sticking spare paper onto the edges of your pattern and trim.

Step 3: Your bodice sewing pattern will now be shorter than the original pattern piece. In order to adjust it to the ideal length, you need to lengthen the bodice just above the waistline by drawing a line across the bodice at a right angle to the centre front line. Cut through the line and spread the pieces apart by the amount you initially shortened the bodice. Stick to some paper and redraw the centre front and side edge lines.

Full bust adjustment (FBA)

There are occasions where creases appear to spread out from the bust that pull across the bodice of a garment or toile. In this situation, when the creases tend to press against the bust, you need to make a full bust adjustment, or FBA, to create more room for the bust. Note that full bust adjustments may not be required in loose-fitting items of clothing.

 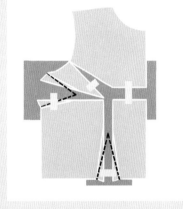

Step 1: Draw a straight line cutting through the bust point at a right angle to the centre front. Then draw a straight line from the curved part of the armhole to the bust point mark. From this new position, draw a line parallel to the centre front down to the lower edge of the bodice (waist position).

Step 2: Cut through the lines and spread the pattern pieces apart by the required amount. Stick the pieces onto a sheet of paper and redraw the darts.

Patterns and cutting layouts

Before you cut out the pattern for any item of clothing you want to sew, identify the line style for your size from the pattern size key. Some sewing patterns use broken or dotted lines of varying weights while others have different-coloured lines. Using a steam-free iron, press out any wrinkles and cut out the paper pattern directly on the inside of the cutting line for your size.

Tip:
Be sure to use paper scissors for this – not your best dressmaking shears!

All your pattern pieces will be labelled with the name of the piece. They will also tell you how many of each piece to cut and how to cut it. For example: back bodice – cut 2; front bodice – cut 1 on the fold.

Every pattern also comes with a cutting layout that shows you how to position the pattern pieces on your fabric and whether the fabric needs to be folded (so that you're cutting two pieces at once) or whether you need to cut individual pieces from a single layer of fabric. The cutting layout is designed to enable you to cut the fabric with minimum wastage. There will be a standard layout based on one size as a guidance on how to lay your fabric out.

Before you lay out your fabric, gently press it to remove any kinks and creases. Lay all of your fabric on a flat, smooth surface and ensure the fabric doesn't hang and stretch out of shape.

If the fabric is to be folded, it's usually (but not always) folded lengthways, with the selvedges matching and right sides together. Again, the cutting layout will give you this information. Most pattern pieces include marks that need to be transferred to the fabric (see page 33). Folding the fabric with right sides together means that you can make any marks on the wrong side, so they won't show in the finished garment.

Identify the fabric width for the size of pattern that you're making, fold the fabric as instructed, and lay the paper pattern pieces out on your pressed fabric. Place the pattern pieces face up, with the grainline markings parallel to the grainline of your fabric (see page 31). Lay any pattern pieces that need to be cut on the fold along the folded edge of the fabric. Fit the other pieces in, following the cutting layout.

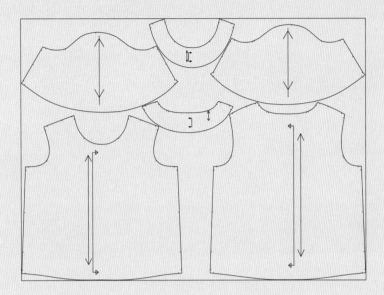

Tip:
Place the pattern piece on the fabric and measure from the selvedge to one end of the pattern grainline. Make a note of the measurement, then pin that end of the pattern grainline to the fabric. Repeat the process at the other end of the pattern grainline, check that the measurement is the same, and then pin that end of the pattern grainline to the fabric. Now you know that the grainline is fixed and won't slip while you pin the rest of the pattern.

Bear in mind, however, that some fabrics need to be 'pattern matched'; if you're using a large checked design, or a pattern with big motifs, then you need to cut it in such a way that the pattern matches across seams. If you're pattern matching, it's best to cut the pieces from a single layer of fabric – but remember to turn the pattern piece over before you cut the second piece so that you cut a mirror image and get a left and a right piece, rather than two lefts! You may also need to buy more fabric than the pattern recommends in order to pattern match.

PINNING AND CUTTING

When you've laid your pattern pieces flat on the fabric, you need to secure them with weights or pins. If you're using pins, then just pin along the long edges of your fabric. Avoid using too many pins – only use enough to keep your paper and fabric in place while cutting (though do note that corners must be pinned well in place to keep the shape intact). If you prefer to use weights, it's a good idea to chalk around the outline of the pattern before you start cutting. Weights are the best option if you're using a very delicate fabric such as silk, where pins would leave marks.

Use a pair of sharp fabric scissors (or a rotary cutter on a self-healing cutting mat) and always cut away from your body; this is not only safer, but also gives you total control of the cutting process. Make sure you cut carefully and slowly, particularly when working around tight corners or small or oddly shaped pattern pieces. This will also reduce the risk of you cutting yourself.

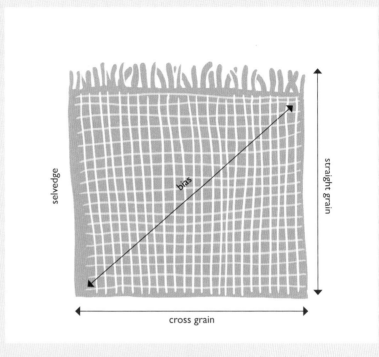

GRAINLINES AND BIAS LINES

Understanding grainlines will help you to get your fabrics to work well for you. Simply put, woven fabrics are created with sets of threads running lengthways and across – these are known as the straight grain (the lengthways threads) and the cross grain. The straight and cross grain threads are always supposed to be at 90 degrees to one another, but from time to time the threads get mismatched. Most pattern pieces are cut on the straight grain, because it is less prone to stretching out of shape and will ensure that your garment hangs properly without any twists. You must line up the straight grain line on your paper pattern pieces with the straight grain of your fabric.

But how do you identify the grain lines and bias lines? To establish the grainline of your fabric, fold it in half so that the two selvedges meet. (The selvedges are the side edges of a piece of fabric; most fabrics have their manufacturing information printed there.) A gentle rip along the edge of your fabric will also help you to find the straight grain when you pull out a weft thread.

Sometimes, pieces need to be cut on the bias. The bias line of a piece of fabric is at 45 degrees to the straight and cross grains. The bias runs diagonally and the fabric stretches the most at the diagonal.

PATTERN MARKINGS

Pattern pieces are marked with various symbols that give you vital information about how to lay out the pattern on the fabric; you will also see symbols that need to be transferred to the fabric pieces, as they relate to how the garment is put together.

Straight grain: This line on a sewing pattern should be placed along the straight grain of your fabric (see page 31).

'Place on fold' line: This symbol indicates that the pattern piece should be placed exactly on the fold of the fabric, so that you cut a piece that's perfectly symmetrical.

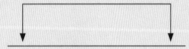

Notches: These triangular symbols indicate where one fabric piece needs to be matched to another – for example, a sleeve to an armhole.

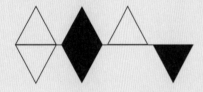

Darts: Darts are used to shape a garment (see page 39), and these marks show where they should be sewn.

Adjustment lines: These marks are included on some pattern pieces to indicate where you can lengthen or shorten a piece without disturbing the balance of the design.

TRANSFERRING PATTERN MARKINGS

After you've cut out your fabric pieces but before you remove the paper patterns, it is extremely important to transfer markings such as notches, darts and buttonhole positions to the fabric pieces.

Notches

Some notches are single and some are double – for example, a single notch is used to mark the front of a sleeve and armhole, while a double notch marks the back. When you sew the pieces together, you must make sure you match them up correctly for a good fit.

To mark a notch, you can cut a small snip using the tip of your scissors. (Make sure you do not cut beyond the seam allowance, which is usually 1.5cm/⅝in from the edge of the piece). Alternatively, cut around the outside edge of the notch mark when you cut out the fabric piece.

Darts

To transfer dart markings, simply place a sheet of dressmaker's carbon paper between your paper pattern and the fabric, with the chalk side of the carbon paper facing the wrong side of your fabric, and run a tracing wheel along the dart lines. This will transfer the marks on your fabric, ready for sewing.

Circles

Circles are used on pattern to show the position of buttonholes, belt loops, pockets and so on. Push a pin through the pattern to the wrong side of your fabric and then use chalk or a fabric marker pen to make a mark on that side.

Get sewing

When your pieces are cut out, and all the marks have been transferred onto the wrong side of your fabric, it's time to get sewing!

At this point it's worth doing a test run on a small double-layered swatch of the fabric you're using, because in most cases you'll be stitching two pieces of fabric together to form a seam. This helps to ensure that you have chosen the right needle for your fabric and that you have set the correct stitch length and thread tension on your machine; with the wrong thread tension, you could end up with a loose or extremely tight seam.

Once you have tested your swatch and made any necessary adjustments, you are ready to start sewing your pieces. Always place your pieces together with wrong sides facing each other and with any notches matching with each other. Pin your fabric pieces together.

DIFFERENT KINDS OF STITCHES

Here are a few basic stitches that you will come across time and time again.

Apart from the usual straight stitches and some decorative stitches, sewing machines come with some other essential stitches. Zig-zag stitches, or lightning stitches if your machine has that function – not all do – are essential for sewing stretchy fabrics because they enable the fabric to sit beautifully and move with the body without breaking. Lightning stitches are also known as zorro or bolt stitches because they take the shape of lightning bolts. These stitches can be selected using the stitch selection buttons or dial on the front of your machine. How long or wide the stitches need to be depends on the thickness of the fabric or the type of project you are working on; for most medium-weight woven fabrics, you can start with a stitch length of 2.5–3mm, decreasing to 2mm for lighter-weight fabrics such as satin, and increasing for heavier fabrics such as denim. This can be changed using the length and width adjustment buttons or dials on your sewing machine.

Staystitching

Topstitching

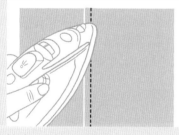

Understitching – Step I

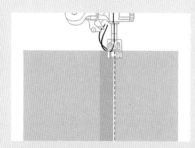

Understitching – Step 2

Edge stitching

Edge stitching is just what it says – stitching on the very edge of the garment. It is visible on the right side of the fabric.

Staystitching

Staystitching is used to stabilize curved fabric edges such as necklines or bias-cut edges to prevent them frowm stretching out of shape. It is done before you begin construction of the garment and is sewn just inside the seam allowance. It can be removed after the proper seam has been sewn.

Topstitching

Topstitching means sewing a line of stitches that will be seen on the right side of the garment. It can be considered a decorative stitch in some cases (for example, a topstitched hem), and a functional stitch in others (for example, when a bias binding is sewn onto a neckline, topstitching closes off the bias binding to secure the raw edges of the neckline).

Understitching

Understitching is used to keep facings (as well as skirt bands and collars) in place and prevent them from rolling out and being visible on the outside of the garment.

Step 1: Sew the facing to the garment, then press both the seam allowances and the facing away from the garment.

Step 2: With the facing uppermost, sew close the seam, stitching through the facing and seam allowances only – not through the external garment piece.

Step 3: Press the facing back down.

Sewing a seam

Before you sew any seams, check your pattern to find out what the seam allowance is. This is the distance from the edge of the fabric to where you stitch. Some sewing machines have measurements on the throat plate that you can use as a guide (consult your manual), but if yours doesn't you can stick down a strip of washi or masking tape instead.

Step 1: Select the pieces that need to be stitched together to create a seam and pin them right sides together along the edges.

Step 2: Thread the machine (consult your manuals for details) and pull long thread tails from both the top thread and the bobbin to the back of the needle. Your machine would be automatically set to a standard 2.5mm, but if yours isn't, remember to adjust it to this stitch length.

Step 3: Raise the presser foot and slide the pinned fabric through the gap between the foot and the throat plate. Using the hand wheel, carefully lower the needle to the point where you want to start sewing. Then lower the presser foot to secure the fabric to the machine. Lightly press the machine pedal with your foot to start sewing.

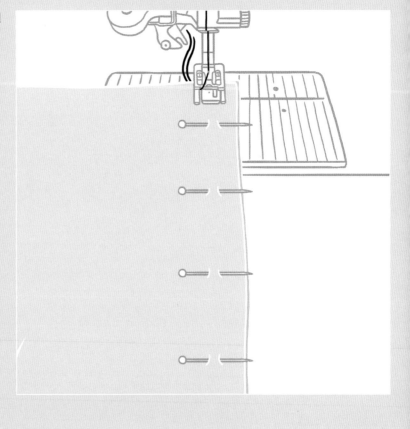

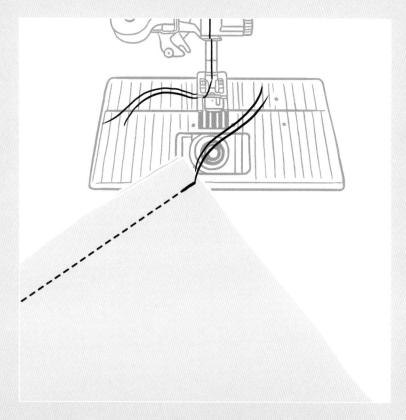

Step 4: After the first three or four stitches, press the reverse stitch lever or button (depending on your machine) and sew three or four backstitches, then release the reverse lever or button to continue with straight stitches. When you get to the end of the seam, backstitch again, then release the lever or button and sew back to the end of your seam to lock the stitches in place and prevent any threads unravelling in the future.

Tip:
When sewing in a straight line, it is easy to focus on the up-and-down movement of the sewing machine needle. Instead, focus on keeping the edge of your fabric along the correct seam allowance mark on your machine.

Step 5: Using thread snips, cut off the thread, leaving a long tail; this avoids you having to rethread the needle before every seam.

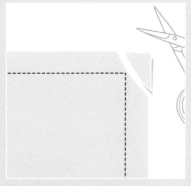

Sewing corners

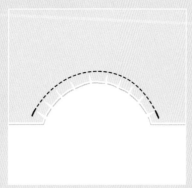

Sewing an inward-curving seam

Sewing an outward-curving seam

SEWING CORNERS AND CURVED SEAMS

Not all pattern pieces have straight lines: some have curves and angles of varying sizes, so it's important to take care in order to produce clean, even seams.

Corners

If you have to turn a corner while sewing, leave the needle in the fabric when you arrive at the corner, raise the presser foot and turn the fabric until the machine foot faces the direction in which you want to continue sewing. Lower the presser foot and continue sewing forwards. This keeps your fabric in place to produce a share point when the fabric is trimmed and turned to the right side.

After sewing a seam that goes around a right-angled corner, you will need to reduce the bulk around the seam allowance to produce a crisp, sharp corner when the garment is turned right side out. To do this, cut off the right angle and trim some of the seam allowance on both sides of the corner. This is especially important if the fabric you are using is particularly bulky. After trimming, turn the garment to the right side and use a blunt-tipped object to carefully push the corner out.

Curves

Whether your edge curves inwards or outwards, use the markings on the plate of the machine as a guide to ensure that your seam allowance remains the same width from start to finish.

After stitching the pieces of fabric together to form a curved seam – for example, around a neckline, an armhole, a princess seam or even a scalloped hems – you will need to either clip the seam allowance to spread out the fabric or notch the seam allowance to fit the seam allowance in, otherwise the curve will not lie flat. Clipping is done on inward curves, such as necklines; it involves cutting small lines into the curve. Bear in mind that the seam could weaken if you clip too much or too close to the stitches.

To cut notches, gently cut little triangular wedges from the seam allowance, again avoiding the stitches.

REDUCING BULK

Often, sewing instructions will tell you to trim, clip or notch the seam allowances after a seam has been sewn. The reason for this is to reduce bulk so that the seam lies flat when the garment is turned through to the right side. Simply use sharp scissors to cut away excess fabric from the seam allowance. We've already seen how to clip corners and notch seams (see opposite), and when it comes to reducing the bulk of a straight seam, simply use sharp scissors to cut away excess fabric from the seam allowance.

SEWING DARTS

Darts are often the first thing that you have to sew when assembling a whole garment. They are used to add shaping around parts of the body such as the bust, hips and waist. They usually come in a triangular shape, with the widest part at the outer edge of the garment, tapering to a point at the end. After stitching, press bust darts downwards and waist darts towards the centre of the garment.

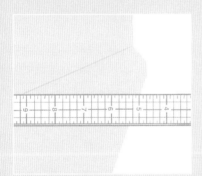

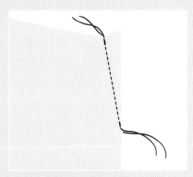

Step 1: Transfer the darts from your sewing pattern to the wrong side of your fabric (see page 33).

Step 2: Fold over the dart legs and pin them in place. Check on both sides of the fabric to ensure that the pin joins the dart legs on both sides.

Step 3: Sew from the edge of your fabric to the dart point, removing the pins as you go. Work a few backstitches at the beginning to secure the dart; at the dart point, tie the top and bobbin threads together to avoid any puckering.

Finishing edges

In most cases, when fabric is cut out, the edges tend to release loose threads that fray and make garments look untidy inside. A few things can be done to stop the fabric from fraying, ranging from the use of pinking shears to the employment of an overlocking machine.

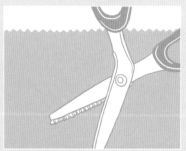

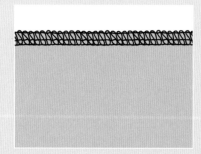

Pinking shears are a special type of scissors with zig-zag cutting edges, which stop fabrics from fraying to some extent because the tiny diagonal cuts are on the bias. They are best used on woven fabrics such as cotton fabric with tight weaves. Fabrics with looser weaves may still fray after pinking shears have been used, so another method should be considered.

The zig-zag sewing machine stitch creates excellent finishes on raw edges. The 'zig-zagging' of the stitches means that the thread wraps around the fibres of the fabric edge and stops them from fraying. Simply set your sewing machine to the zig-zag option and adjust the length to 2.5mm and the width to 3mm. Some sewing machines come with an edge stitching foot, which has a groove to guide the edge of your fabric – but any sewing machine foot with a wide enough gap to allow the zig-zag motion of the needle will work fine. Begin by sewing slowly, so that you can make sure that the zig-zags end at the edge of the fabric.

An overlocker (known as a serger in the US) is a sewing machine with multiple uses. They are able to sew fabric as well as trim off raw edges at the same time. These machines, which use multiple spools of thread simultaneously, give garments a particularly tidy and professional-looking finish.

Tip:
Some sewing machines have an overlock stitch setting that sews a zig-zag in between a few straight stitches in order to resemble overlocker stitches.

PRESSING

Pressing is a vital part of making clothes. Using a good steam iron to lock in stitches and flatten seams sets a homemade item of clothing apart and gives it a professional look. It is advisable to press each seam after it is sewn to remove any puckers, using a plain piece of woven fabric to protect the main garment. To prevent your fabric from getting scorched, ensure that your pressing cloth covers the entire area that the iron will cover.

After sewing a seam, steam press over it to set the stitches into the fibres of your fabric before opening the seam and pressing it again. Most seams are pressed open, but occasionally the instructions will tell you to press the seam to one side.

BIAS BINDING

Bias binding is another effective way to finish off seams by enclosing the raw edges. The technique is most popularly used to finish off necklines and armholes.

Bias tape can be created at home or bought in stores. Double-fold ready-made bias binding comes with crease lines already pressed into it, which means you have a clear stitching line to follow. It's available in many colours and different widths; note that the width stated when you buy it is the width of the strip with both long edges folded in to the centre.

 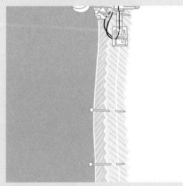 

Step 1: Unfold one of the folds on the bias tape and place it on top of the edge to be bound, with right sides together. Pin the tape in place all the way around; if your edge is a neckline or armhole, leave enough bias tape to be overlapped for a clean finish.

Step 2: Stitching in the fold line, sew the bias tape in place. Backstitch at the beginning and at the end of the seam to prevent it from unravelling

Step 3: If you are working on a circular opening, such as a neckline or armhole, stop a short distance before you get back to your starting point and overlap the ends of the tape. Stitch the overlap and backstitch to secure the stitches.

Step 4: Trim the seam allowance (see page 40). If you're applying binding to a curved edge such as a neckline, clip into the seam allowance along the curve (see page 38), taking care not to cut the stitches.

Step 5: Fold all the bias tape over to the wrong side (roll the seam very slightly to the inside so that it remains invisible) and pin it in place.

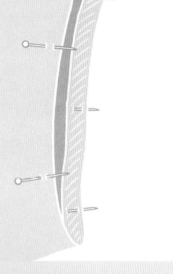

Step 6: Stitching as close as possible to the folded edge of the bias tape, sew along the edge of the bias tape from the right side, making sure that the other side of the bias tape is caught by the stitches.

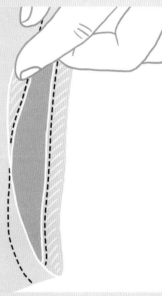

Glossary of essential terms

Backstitching: This is used for securing your stitches to make sure that your stitched seams do not unravel (also known as lockstitching). It should be done at the beginning and at the end of a seam. After the first and last four stitches at every seam, press and hold the backstitch function on your sewing machine whilst pressing down the foot pedal of the machine. Sew four stitches backwards, release the backstitch button function and sew four stitches forward.

Basting: Also known as tacking, this is the stitching of long (4/5mm) temporary stitches that are done to stitch two fabric pieces together temporarily in order to keep them together whilst performing other tasks. Basting can be done with a sewing machine or by hand using hand-sewing needles.

Clipping and trimming: After sewing curved seams, small cuts have to be made into the seam allowances to enable the seam on the finished garment to lay flat. It gives a professional finish to garments but must be done with care by using small scissors to avoid cutting into the seams.

Facing: Using pieces of fabric to finish raw edges by sewing them to a garment and turning them under.

Finishing seams: A range of methods used for neatening the raw edges on the inside of seams, which could include the use of pinking shears, zigzagging with a sewing machine or using an overlocking machine. Many other finishing techniques exist including lining, which involves adding a second layer of fabric inside the main garment fabric that sits next to the skin.

Gathering: A method of adding fullness to a garment achieved by sewing two parellel rows of long (4/5mm) stitches. By pulling the long, top thread tails left at each end of the fabric, the fabric creases and 'gathers' along these lines. A new, final line of stitches is sewn to hold the gathers in place, often done when the gathered edge is sewn to another pattern piece, and the temporary gathering stitches are removed.

Hemming: A method for finishing garments. The hems of different garments vary and can be identified on the sewing pattern piece. When marking on the fabric, it is important to use a measuring gauge as you fold over and press the hem to ensure that the garment hangs beautifully and evenly all around.

Interfacing: A stabilizing piece of cloth that is attached to the wrong side of your garment fabric to add support or firmness to an area. It is typically ironed on or stitched on to the wrong side of the fabric.

Seam allowance: The distance between the stitching line and the edge of the fabric pieces you are about to sew. In this book, we will be using the standard 1.5cm ($\frac{5}{8}$in) seam allowance unless otherwise stated.

Selvedge: The factory-finished side edge of a piece of fabric, which does not fray.

Staystitching: An extremely important technique to avoid stretching and give your creations a professional finish. It is done by sewing straight stitches just inside a seam allowance.

Topstitching: A row of stitches visible from the right side of a garment. It is used as a design feature or for the extra stability of a seam.

Understitching: This is very important for stopping facings or linings from gaping from the wrong side of a garment. It is done by stitching the seam allowance through the lining or facing and has to be done very close to the stitching line – usually 3mm ($\frac{1}{8}$in).

Scan here to download the patterns for all of the projects.

Projects

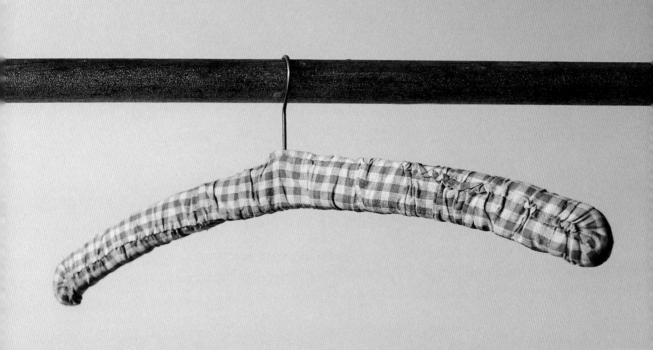

NOTE
A 1.5cm (⅝in) seam allowance is used throughout unless otherwise specified. For a clean, professional look, finish the raw edges of the fabric as you work (see page 40), using your preferred method.

June top

Light- to medium-weight woven
  fabric of your choice (for amount,
  see below)
50cm (20in) very lightweight iron-on
  (fusible) interfacing
Matching sewing machine thread
Basic sewing kit (see page 10)

If you're new to dressmaking, this simple T-shirt-style top is a great project
to start with. It consists of only five pieces and is made in a lightweight
woven fabric, which is the easiest fabric to sew with as it can withstand a lot
of handling without stretching out of shape. It also gives you the chance to
practice several essential techniques: finishing edges, sewing seams and hems,
and attaching a neckline facing. The latter might sound tricky – but as long as
you take your time, it's actually less fiddly than trying to turn under a neat,
very narrow hem.

GARMENT SIZE	6	8	10	12	14	16	18	20	22	24	26	28
FABRIC QUANTITY (M)	1	1.01	1.02	1.05	1.07	1.08	1.12	1.17	1.23	1.45	1.53	1.6
FABRIC QUANTITY (YD)	1⅛	1⅛	1⅛	1¼	1¼	1¼	1¼	1⅓	1⅜	1⅝	1¾	1¾

FABRIC SUGGESTIONS
Look for fabrics with some softness
and drape, such as lightweight
cotton and cotton blends, linens and
linen blends, viscose/rayon, crepe
or voile. You will need extra fabric
in order to match stripes, plaids or
fabrics with one-way designs.

PATTERN INVENTORY

1. **Front bodice** cut 1 on the fold from fabric

2. **Back bodice** cut 1 on the fold from fabric

3. **Sleeve** cut 1 pair from fabric

4. **Front neckline facing** cut 1 on the fold from fabric and
    1 on the fold from interfacing

5. **Back neckline facing** cut 1 on the fold from fabric and
    1 on the fold from interfacing

Project continues overleaf

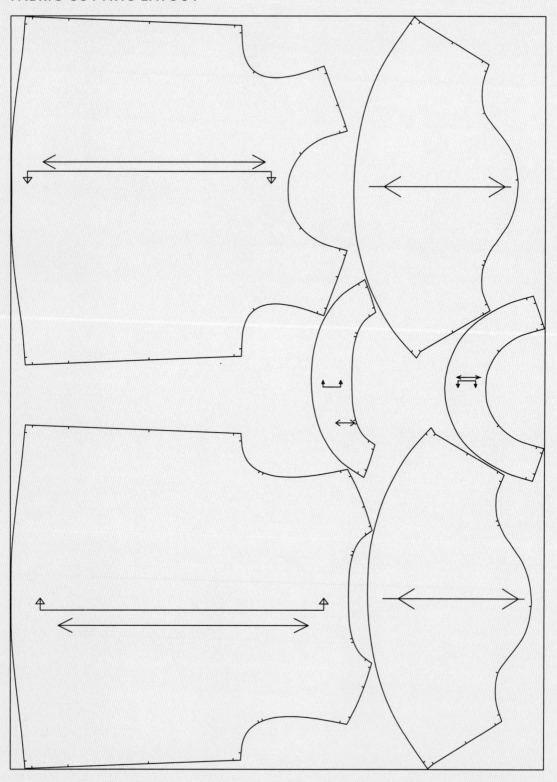

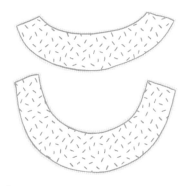

2

PREPARE THE PIECES

1. Prepare and press your fabric (see page 19). Cut out the fabric pieces, then transfer all pattern markings to the fabric (see page 33).

2. Following the manufacturer's instructions, apply interfacing to the wrong side of the front and back neckline facings.

3. Finish the raw edges of all pieces (see page 40), except for the curved necklines.

SEW THE BODICE

4. With right sides together and notches matching, pin the front and back bodices together at the shoulder seams. Sew together, then press the seams open.

5. Lay the bodice out flat. With right sides together and notches matching, pin the sleeves to the armholes.

4

Project continues overleaf

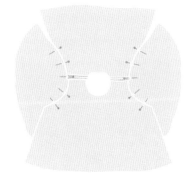

5

6

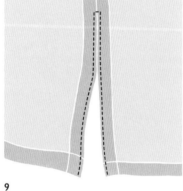

9

6. Sew the sleeves in place, lightly easing them into the armholes at the sleeve cap. Press the seam allowances towards the bodice.

7. Attach the neckline facing (see *Essential skill: Attaching a neckline facing*, opposite).

8. Fold the bodice in half at the shoulders, with right sides together and notches matching. Starting at the end of the sleeves, pin and sew the underarm and side seams on each side in one continuous line of stitching, stopping at the side slit notches.

9. Press the side seams open, pressing the unstitched seam allowances to the wrong sides along the side slits. Starting from the bottom, sew up the side slit, stitching along the seam allowance fold line; at the top of the slit, with the needle still in the fabric, raise the presser foot and pivot the fabric, then sew down the other side of the fold.

10. Fold and press the bottom edge of the top to the wrong side by 2.5cm (1in) and then by 2.5cm (1in) again. Sew close to the open edge, using a 3mm stitch length.

11. Hem the bottom edges of the sleeves in the same way, then give your top a final press.

Project continues overleaf

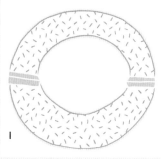

Essential skill

ATTACHING A NECKLINE FACING

Facings are used not only to provide extra support in certain areas of garments, but also to finish and conceal raw edges. In this project, facings are sewn around the neckline. The seam allowances have to be trimmed, clipped and understitched so that they will remain in place.

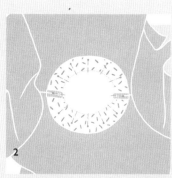

1. With right sides together, pin the front and back neckline facings together at the shoulders. Sew together, then press the seams open.

2. Lay the top out flat, right side up, with the facing right side down around the neckline, making sure that the shoulder seams and notches match. Pin in place.

3. Using a 1cm (⅜in) seam allowance, carefully sew around the curved neckline.

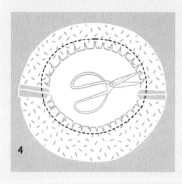

4. Now you need to reduce the bulk around the neckline and eliminate any 'bunching up' of the fabric beneath the neckline. Either trim the seam allowance as close as possible to the stitching line or clip into the curved neckline, as shown here, avoiding the stitches.

5. Carefully press the clipped or trimmed seam allowance away from the bodice.

6. Understitch (see page 35) the trimmed or clipped seam allowance to the facing. This helps the edge of the neckline to sit perfectly as you press the neckline in place. Understitching should be done as close to the stitching line as possible, but it should not be visible on the right side of the garment.

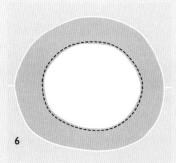

June dress variation

Once you've mastered the top, why not try your hand at this variation? You can use the same pattern to create a simple dress, which you can make as short or as long as you wish.

YOU WILL NEED
Your chosen fabric (see below for amount, plus extra for the skirt; see overleaf)
50cm (20in) very lightweight iron-on (fusible) interfacing
Matching sewing machine thread
Basic sewing kit (see page 10)

GARMENT SIZE	6	8	10	12	14	16	18	20	22	24	26	28
FABRIC QUANTITY (M)	1	1.01	1.02	1.05	1.07	1.08	1.12	1.17	1.23	1.45	1.53	1.6
FABRIC QUANTITY (YD)	1⅛	1⅛	1⅛	1¼	1¼	1¼	1¼	1⅓	1⅜	1⅝	1¾	1¾

FABRIC SUGGESTIONS
As with the top, look for fabrics with some softness and drape, such as lightweight cotton and cotton blends, linens and linen blends, viscose/rayon, crepe or voile.

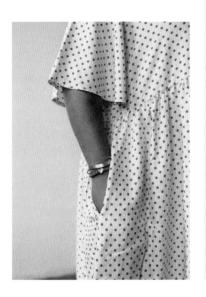

PATTERN INVENTORY

1. **Front bodice** cut 1 on the fold from fabric

2. **Back bodice** cut 1 on the fold from fabric

3. **Sleeve** cut 1 pair from fabric

4. **Front facing** cut 1 on the fold from fabric and 1 on the fold from interfacing

5. **Back facing** cut 1 on the fold from fabric and 1 on the fold from interfacing

Project continues overleaf

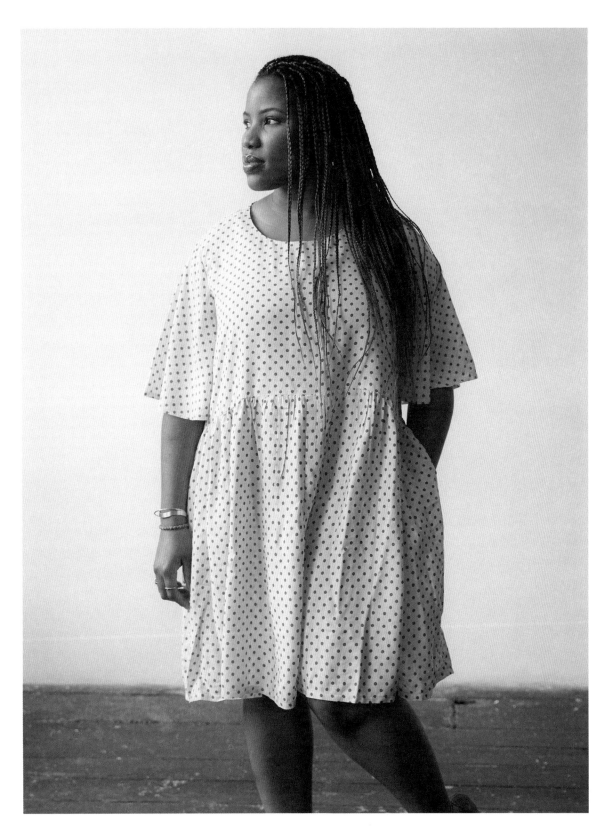

You don't need a pattern piece for the bottom half of your dress, as it's just a rectangle of fabric that's gathered and eased into the bodice.

- To work out the width of the piece of fabric you need to cut, measure around the widest part of your hips and use this calculation:

- **For a full skirt:** Multiply your hip measurement by 2.5.

- **For a skirt with medium gathers:** Multiply your hip measurement by 2.

- **For a lightly gathered skirt:** Multiply your hip measurement by 1.5.

The length of your skirt is totally up to you – just add 1.5cm (⅝in) to the length you want the finished skirt to be to allow for the seam allowance at the top (where you attach the skirt to the bodice) and the hem at the bottom.

PREPARE THE PIECES

1. Prepare and press your fabric (see page 19). Cut out all the paper pattern pieces except the front and back bodices. Note that there is a new waistline to cut out (different from the June top). After cutting out the paper pattern, pin them to your fabric and cut the fabric out for the dress.

SEW THE DRESS BODICE

2. Sew the bodice, following steps 1–8 of the June top, this time stitching all the way down the side seams, as there are no side slits. Press the side seams open, then set the bodice aside.

SEW THE SKIRT

1. Fold the rectangle of fabric for the skirt in half lengthways, with right sides together. Pin and sew the short sides together. Press the seam open.

2. Finish the bottom raw edge of the skirt (see page 40). Press.

3. Gather the top edge of the skirt (see *Essential skill: Sewing gathers*, page 63). The gathered fabric should measure the same as the circumference of the top.

4. With right sides together, pin the bottom edge of the top over the gathered edge of the skirt. Sew in place. Finish the raw edge using your preferred method (see page 40). Press the seam up, towards the bodice.

HEM THE DRESS

5. Fold the bottom edge of the dress to the wrong side by 2.5cm (1in) and stitch in place. Give your dress a press and enjoy!

Jola tiered skirt

YOU WILL NEED

Light to medium-weight woven
    fabric (for amount, see below)
Matching sewing machine thread
Contrasting sewing machine thread
Elastic (enough to fit around your
    waist) 2.5cm (1in) wide
Basic sewing kit (see page 10)
Safety pin or bodkin

Gathers look impressive, but they couldn't be easier to stitch – perfect for beginners. Here, they're the main feature of a flamboyant three-tiered maxi skirt that sits high on the waist and flares out at the hem. Style it with a simple top and leather sandals for a timeless look – and because the gathers hide a multitude of sins, you don't even need to worry too much if your stitching's a bit wonky!

GARMENT SIZE	6	8	10	12	14	16	18	20	22	24	26	28
FABRIC QUANTITY (M)	1.59	1.95	1.95	1.95	1.95	1.95	1.95	2.31	2.31	2.31	2.31	2.31
FABRIC QUANTITY (YD)	1¾	1⅞	1⅞	1⅞	1⅞	1⅞	1⅞	2½	2½	2½	2½	2½

FABRIC SUGGESTIONS

Opt for light- to medium-weight fabrics with subtle drape and movement, such as lightweight cotton, viscose/rayon, gingham, voile, georgette or soft linen. As well as being a perfect sewing pattern for all-over print fabrics, this design is also ideal for mixing and matching contrast prints, textures and colours.

PATTERN INVENTORY

1. **Top tier** cut 1 pair on the fold

2. **Middle tier** cut 1 pair on the fold

3. **Bottom tier** cut 1 pair on the fold

Project continues overleaf

FABRIC CUTTING LAYOUT

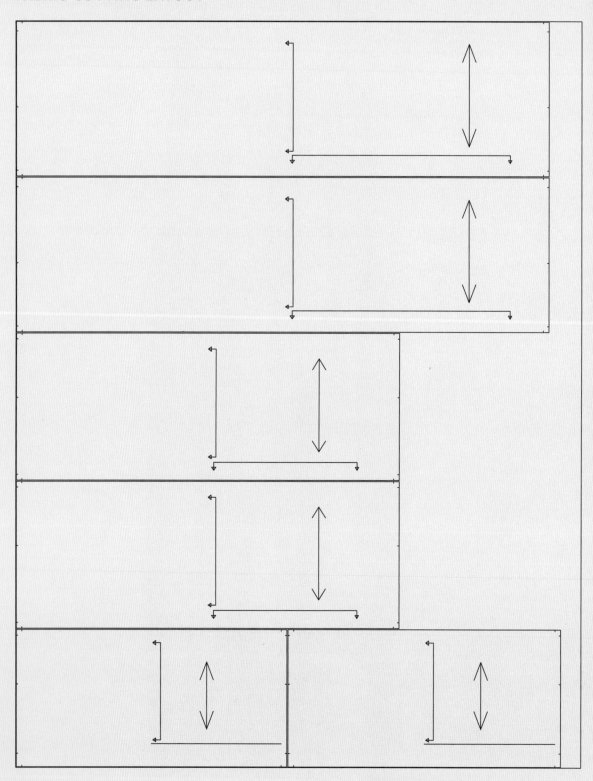

Tip:
Separate the pieces for each tier to avoid getting confused further down the line. It's a good idea to label them with post-it notes or colour code them using different-coloured pins.

4

Note:
Sample cutting layout for size 18 on 150cm (60in) fabric width on the fold.

PREPARE THE PIECES

1. Prepare and press your fabric (see page 19). Cut out the pieces, transferring all pattern markings to the fabric (see page 33).

SEW THE SKIRT PANELS

2. With right sides together, matching the notches, pin and sew the short ends of the top tier panels together to form a loop. Finish raw edges of the side seams (see page 40) and press the seams open. Repeat with the middle and bottom tiers.

3. Around the top edge of the top panel, fold over and press 1cm (⅜in) to the wrong side. Fold over a further 2.5cm (1in), press and pin in place.

4. Sew around the channel as close as possible to the edge of the fold, stopping about 8cm (3in) before the end to create a gap to pass the elastic through.

How much elastic should I cut?

With a measuring tape, measure your waist or around the position where you prefer your skirts to sit. Subtract 5cm (2in) from the waist measurement; that figure is the length of elastic you need to cut. For example, a woman with a waist measurement of 86cm (34in) would need to cut a strip of elastic 81cm (32in) long.

5. Cut the elastic to the required length (see above) and attach a safety pin or bodkin to one end. Insert the pin or bodkin into the gap and feed it around the channel, taking care not to twist the elastic as you do so. Remember that the elastic will be much shorter than the elastic waist channel of your skirt – so as the elastic passes through, pin the other end of the elastic band onto the fabric to avoid losing the elastic inside the channel.

Project continues overleaf

6

Tip:
As an optional extra to step 7, to stop wide bands of elastic from twisting in the channel, you can sew over the waist channel. To do this, stitch through the elastic using a long stitch length. Remember to stretch the elastic as you sew.

6. Once the elastic has gone all around the channel, overlap the ends and pin them together. Switch your sewing machine setting to a zig-zag stitch, then sew back and forth over the elastic a few times to secure it in place.

7. Switch your machine back to normal straight stitch. Pin and sew the gap in the waist channel closed, following the original stitch line.

GATHER THE TIERS AND ASSEMBLE THE SKIRT

8. Gather the top edges of the middle and bottom tiers (see *Essential skill: Sewing gathers*, opposite).

9. With right sides together, making sure the seams match, pin the bottom edge of tier 1 and the top edge of tier 2 together. You will need to ease the gathered top edge of tier 2 into the bottom edge of tier 1 by carefully tugging or loosening the gathering stitches as necessary. When both edges match, sew the pieces together with the gathered side on top, to ensure that the gathers are fed evenly through your machine. Take a 1.5cm (⅝in) seam allowance, which should be shy of your second row of gathering stitches. Unpick the contrasting gathering stitches and finish the raw edge using your preferred method (see page 40). Press the seam down.

Project continues overleaf

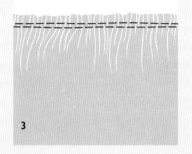

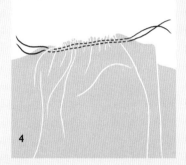

SEWING GATHERS

Gathers are essential for building texture, fullness and movement into garments. In addition to serving as a design feature, gathers are also used to fit larger pieces of fabric into smaller spaces, allowing for effective shaping to accommodate curves etc. There are many ways to gather fabric, but for the projects in this book we will use the traditional method of sewing rows of gathering stitches.

1. Adjust the stitch length on your sewing machine to the longest stitch, which is usually about 4mm long (check your sewing machine manual).

2. With the right side facing up, using contrasting-coloured thread, sew a row of stitches inside the seam allowance. The patterns in this book have a 1.5cm (⅝in) seam allowance, so your first row of stitches should be about 1cm (⅜in) away from the raw edge. Leave a long tail of threads at both ends of the stitching; you do not need to backstitch.

3. Sew a second row of stitches parallel to the first, still within the seam allowance, a fraction away from the first row; use the width of the presser foot as a guide.

4. From the wrong side, pull on the bottom threads (also known as the bobbin threads). Slide the fabric along until it is the correct length. Adjust by sliding the fabric back and forth until you have the correct measurement. Wrap the threads around a pin to secure them.

5. Set your sewing machine stitch length back to the standard length and sew between the gathering stitches, carefully feeding the gathers through. This step and the next may be completed as you join the gathered piece to another.

6. Unpick the gathering stitches and remove the threads.

10. Attach the top of the bottom tier to the bottom of the middle tier in the same way.

<u>Pressing gathers</u>

I have found that gathers behave differently depending on which way you press them. When the seams are pressed up, the gathers look flatter than they would when the seams are pressed downwards. Pressing the seam downwards subtly 'pouffes' out the gathers.

HEM THE SKIRT

11. With all three tiers stitched together, you will be left with an unfinished edge – the hem at the base of your skirt. Fold over and press 1cm (⅜in) to the wrong side, followed by a further 1.5cm (⅝in), and pin in place. Sew as close as you can to the fold. Give the skirt a steam press to finish.

Jola skirt variations

- Lengthen or shorten any of the tiers to get skirts of varying-lengths.

- Omit either the middle or bottom tier for a midi-length skirt. Note that if the middle tier is eliminated, then the gathers attached to the top tier will have a very full, poufy effect.

Jenny sweatshirt

YOU WILL NEED
Knit fabric of your choice (for
    amount, see below)
70cm (27½in) rib fabric
Matching sewing machine thread
Basic sewing kit (see page 10)
Ballpoint sewing machine needle
Sewing machine walking foot
    (optional)

The Jenny sweatshirt is a good introduction to sewing with knit/stretchy fabrics, which need to be handled slightly differently to the woven fabrics we've used so far because – you guessed it! – they stretch. With its relaxed fit, classic long sleeves and ribbed crew neck and cuffs, it's very easy to slip on and off. It has an asymmetrical cut across the front and back, which lends itself perfectly to colour blocking. Pair it with jeans or dress it down with coordinating lounge bottoms for a cosy, monochromatic look. Alternatively, size up your pattern for an oversized fit.

GARMENT SIZE	6	8	10	12	14	16	18	20	22	24	26	28
FABRIC QUANTITY (M)	1.04	1.1	1.14	1.22	1.24	1.28	1.31	1.33	1.39	1.47	1.54	1.65
FABRIC QUANTITY (YD)	1¼	1¼	1¼	1⅓	1⅜	1½	1½	1½	1⅝	1⅝	1¾	1⅞

FABRIC SUGGESTIONS
Select knit or jersey fabrics such as sweatshirt fabric, fleece, French terry, interlock and other jersey or knit fabrics with at least 15 percent stretch.

PATTERN INVENTORY

1. **Top front panel** cut 1 from main fabric (wrong side up)

2. **Lower front panel** cut 1 from main fabric (wrong side up)

3. **Top back panel** cut 1 from main fabric (right side up)

4. **Lower back panel** cut 1 from main fabric (right side up)

5. **Sleeve** cut 1 pair from main fabric (any side up)

6. **Neckband** cut 1 on the fold from rib fabric

7. **Cuff** cut 2 on the fold from rib fabric

Project continues overleaf

FABRIC CUTTING LAYOUT

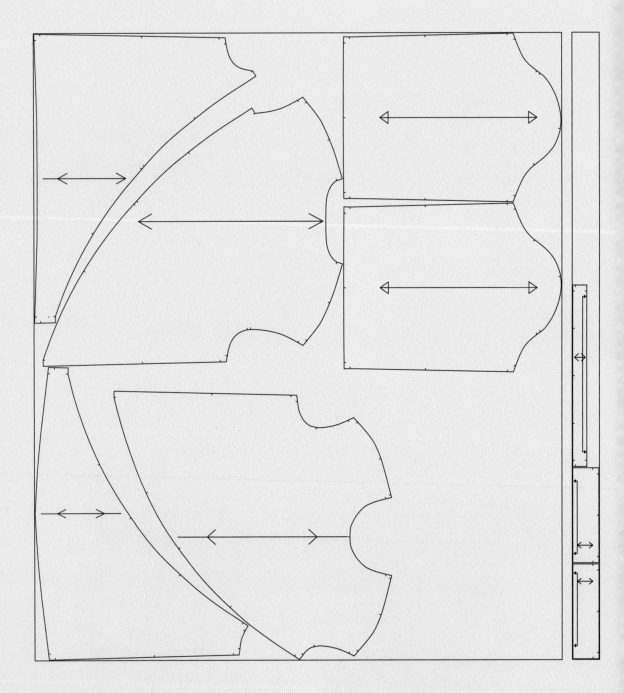

WORKING WITH KNIT/STRETCHY FABRICS

Knit fabrics are stretchy by nature. If they are sewn in the same way as woven fabrics, then the threads are likely to snap – especially in areas that get stretched when worn. So there are two important things to remember when it comes to sewing with knit fabrics: you need to use both a different kind of stitch and a different kind of needle.

Regular sewing machine needles have a sharp point, which could split and break the fibres of your stretchy fabric. Instead, you need to use a ballpoint needle, which has a slightly rounded tip that will separate the fibres rather than pierce them.

Sewing stretch fabrics with a regular straight stitch can result in broken stitches, so take the time to study your sewing machine manual and identify which stitches are recommended for stretchy fabrics (often stretch stitches, which are also known as lightning stitches). Alternatively, switch to a small zig-zag stitch: adjust the stitch length to 2.5–3mm and the stitch width 1–1.5mm; this will allow your knit fabric to stretch with ease and look neat on the right side. It's worth taking the time to do a test run using a swatch of your main fabric; you should also check whether your sewing machine presser foot is open and wide enough for the zig-zag movement of the needle.

Project continues overleaf

Note:
Sample cutting layout for size 18 on 150cm (60in) fabric width on the fold.

2

PREPARE THE PIECES

1. Prepare and press your fabric (see page 19). Pay close attention to the cutting instructions so that you know which side of the fabric should be facing up or down. Do not fold the fabric before you cut the front and back sweatshirt panels (1–4); do fold it before you cut out the sleeves, cuffs and band (5–7). Cut out the pieces, transferring all pattern markings to the fabric (see page 33).

JOIN THE TOP AND LOWER PANELS

2. With right sides together, match the notches along the base of the top front panel to the notches along the top edge of the lower front panel. Taking care not to overstretch the fabric, pin the panels together and sew from one end to the other.

3. If the raw edges of your fabric do not need to be finished, trim a little bit off the seam allowance and press the seam down towards the hem of the sweatshirt. Alternatively, finish the raw edge using your sewing machine's zig-zag function. An optional step is to topstitch (see page 35) the seam allowances to the lower front panel. For this, you can use either a twin needle or a zig-zag stitch. If you opt for zig-zag stitches, the width and length should be the same – for example, 2.5mm width and 2.5mm length.

4. Repeat steps 2 and 3 with the top and lower back panels.

SEW THE SHOULDER SEAMS

5. With right sides together, matching the notches, lay the back of the sweatshirt on top of the front. Pin and sew the shoulder seams. Trim or finish the seam allowances, then press the seams open.

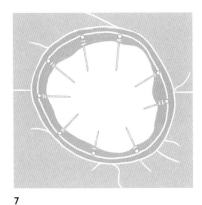

7

Tip:
To find the mid-point, fold the sweatshirt in half at the neckline and mark it with a pin.

10

Tip:
If rib fabric is used for the neckband and cuffs, I do not recommend trimming at this point because they fray – a lot! Therefore, take some time to finish the raw edge of the neckline so that your sweatshirt will last through many wash cycles in its lifetime.

ATTACH THE NECKBAND

6. The neckband is made up of a single piece of rib fabric. Fold the fabric in half lengthways and stitch the short ends together. Press the seam open.

7. Fold the neckband in half widthways, with wrong sides together. Lay the sweatshirt out on a flat surface and pin the folded neckband around the right side of the neckline, aligning the raw edges. The neckband seam should lie exactly at the mid-point of the back neckline. Match all the other notches on the neckband to the correct point on the sweatshirt – centre back (CB), the two side seams (SS) and centre front (CF). You will notice that the neckband is smaller than the neckline: stretch it to fit around the neckline and pin in place.

8. Carefully sew from the centre back all around the neckband.

9. Neaten the raw edge using an overlocker or a sewing machine zig-zag stitch (a 3-step zig-zag function is ideal if your machine has one).

10. With the new seam allowance around the neckline facing towards the body, topstitch the seam allowance to the neckline.

Project continues overleaf

13

INSERT THE SLEEVES

11. With your sweatshirt lying opened out flat, with right sides together, place the sleeve pieces around the armholes. Take time to check that you have matched the notches correctly – the double notches for the back of the sleeves should match the double notches on the back armhole.

12. Pin the sleeves to the armholes and sew in place. Trim or finish the seam allowance and press the seam allowance towards the sleeves.

SEW THE SIDE SEAMS

13. Fold the sweatshirt at the shoulders, right sides together, matching the sleeve and side seam notches. Pin in place, then sew from the end of the sleeve to the armhole and down the side seam in one continuous line.

14. Trim the seam allowance or finish it using an overlocker or sewing machine zig-zag stitch. Press the seam open. Repeat steps 13 and 14 on the other side of the sweatshirt.

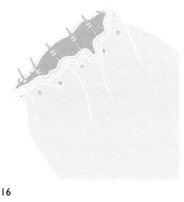

SEW THE CUFFS

15. Fold the cuffs in half widthways, right sides together, to form a rectangle with the fold at the top. Pin and sew the short edges at the end of each rectangle together, then press the seams open. Now fold the cuff in half lengthways; do not press.

16. Slide a cuff into the right side of one sleeve, matching the sleeve and cuff seams and notches and aligning the raw edges. Stretch, ease and pin the cuff to the sleeve. Sew the cuff in place. Finish the raw edges and press the seam open. Repeat with the other sleeve.

16

HEM THE SWEATSHIRT

17. Finish the raw edge around the hem (this is not necessary if your fabric does not fray). Measure and fold over a 2.5cm (1in) hem to the wrong side. Press and pin the fold in place. Topstitch (see page 35) close to the fabric edge using either twin needles, your regular sewing machine zig-zag or lightning stitch.

18. Give your sweatshirt a steam press to shrink it back in place after all the tugging and manipulation.

Jenny sweatshirt variations

- Add a waistband.

- Add an iron-on vinyl.

- Add some hand-embroidered details.

- Use the same or contrasting coloured fabric for the panels.

Joy pinafore dress

YOU WILL NEED

Medium- to heavy-weight woven
  fabric of your choice (for amount,
  see below)
50cm (20in) very lightweight iron-
  on (fusible) interfacing
Matching sewing machine thread
36cm (14in) closed-end zip
4m (4.3yd) double-fold ready-
  made 13mm (½in) bias binding
Small hook-and-eye closure
Basic sewing kit (see page 10)

This project is all about creating neat finishes and closures. The neckline and cross-over back panels are edged with bias binding – a technique that comes in handy for so many sewing projects, from comfy cushions to couture creations. It also features a centred zip – the simplest and most common of all zip closures, and a technique that's an essential part of every dressmaker's arsenal of skills. This is a stylish and feminine dress that's a great addition to your wardrobe. It can be paired with a casual T-shirt or, for a smarter look, a crisp, elegant shirt.

GARMENT SIZE	6	8	10	12	14	16	18	20	22	24	26	28
FABRIC QUANTITY (M)	1.7	1.74	1.78	1.85	1.92	2.02	2.17	2.27	2.33	2.41	2.48	2.5
FABRIC QUANTITY (YD)	1⅞	2	2	2	2⅛	2¼	2⅜	2½	2⅝	2⅔	2¾	2¾

FABRIC SUGGESTIONS

Use mid-weight to slightly heavier, zero-stretch cotton blend fabrics, gabardine, denim, lightweight wool blends or linen blend fabrics. Whatever fabric you choose will need to have good opacity to hide the bias tape. Choose a simple block colour or small-scale prints.

PATTERN INVENTORY

1. **Front bodice** cut 1 on the fold from fabric

2. **Back bodice** cut 1 pair from fabric

3. **Front skirt** cut 1 on the fold from fabric

4. **Back skirt** cut 1 on the fold from fabric

5. **Back waistband** cut 2 on the fold from fabric and 2 on the fold from interfacing

6. **Front waistband** cut 2 on the fold from fabric and 2 on the fold from interfacing

Project continues overleaf

FABRIC CUTTING LAYOUT

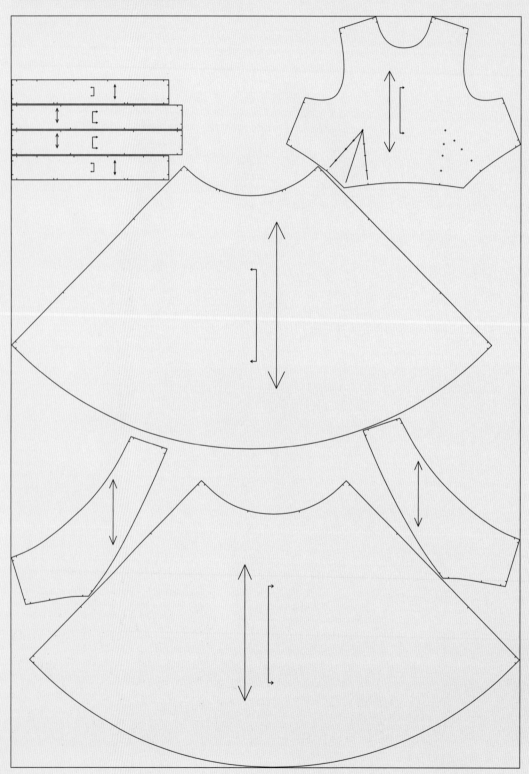

Note:
Sample cutting
layout for size 18 on
150cm (60in) fabric
width on the fold.

PREPARE THE PIECES

1. Prepare and press your fabric (see page 19). Cut out the pieces, transferring all pattern markings to the fabric (see page 33). Following the manufacturer's instructions, apply interfacing to the wrong side of the front and back waistband pieces.

2. Staystitch (see page 35) the front bodice neckline and the curved horizontal edges of the back bodice panels.

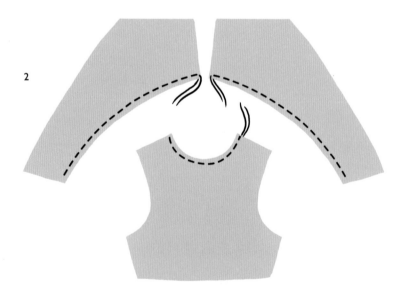

SEW THE FRONT AND BACK BODICE PANELS

3. On the wrong side of the front bodice, pin and sew the waist darts (see page 39) . Press the darts towards the side.

4. With right sides together, match the front and back bodice panels at the shoulder seam lines. Pin and sew the shoulder seams. Finish the raw edges (see page 40) and press the shoulder seams open.

5. With right sides together, cross the left back bodice over to the right-hand side of the front at the side seam. Pin and sew in place, then press the seam open. Pin the right back bodice to the left-hand side of the front in the same way, but do not stitch.

6. Finish the raw side seam edges and press the seam open. Turn the bodice right side out. Finish the raw edges of the unstitched left side seam.

Project continues overleaf

3

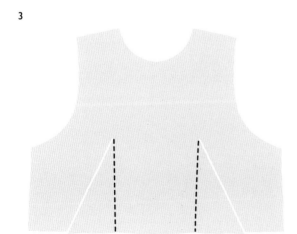

5

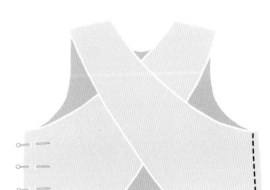

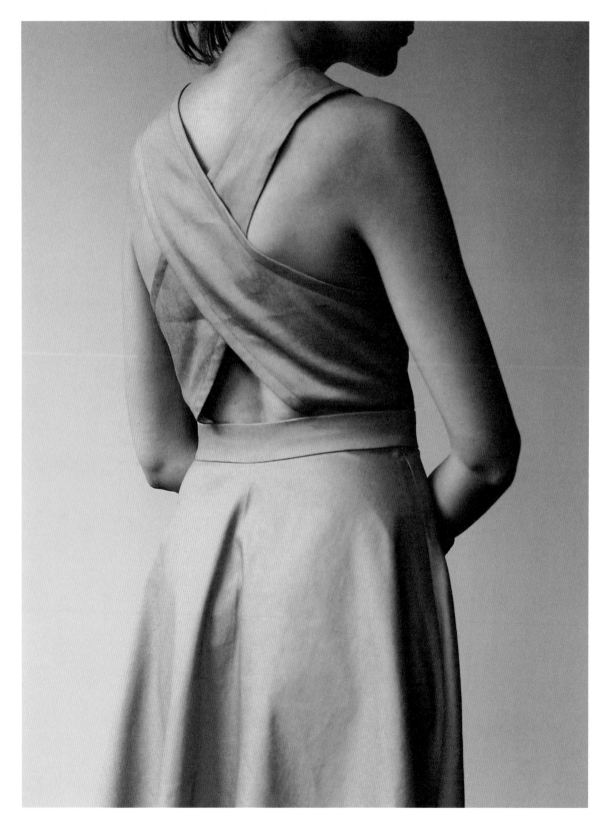

PROJECTS

7

8

FINISH THE NECKLINE, ARMHOLES AND BACK PANEL RAW EDGES

Now that the shoulder seams have been stitched together, you will have very long raw edges from one side of the bodice to the other. You will use bias binding to finish those edges. You will need a very long strip of bias tape, which should not be visible on the right side of your pinafore once this stage is completed.

7. With right sides together, pin the bias tape all around the staystitched neckline edges of the front and back panels. Stitch it in place, starting 20cm (8in) away from the front and back left side seams; the bias tape will later be used to conceal the top edge of the zip tape, so you need to leave part of it unstitched for now. The other raw-edged end of the back panel will be bound before the skirt waistband is sewn in place.

8. Pin bias tape around the armholes and the other edge of the back panels. You will need to do this in two stages; from left back panel around the right armhole, and from right back panel around left armhole. Stitch in place.

Project continues overleaf

<u>Tip:</u>
The heavier-weight fabric I have used to make the Joy pinafore dress means that the bias binding in steps 7 and 8 does not require understitching to hold it in place. If you use a different, lighter fabric, understitching might be required.

11

MAKE UP THE FRONT AND BACK SKIRTS

9. Finish the raw edges of the front and back skirt side seams. With right sides together, pin and sew the front and back skirts together along the right-hand side seam. (The left-hand side will be sewn when the waistbands are completed.)

ATTACH THE WAISTBAND

10. Place one front waistband and one back waistband right sides together. Pin and sew the right-hand side seam. Press the seam open; this piece will now be referred to as the outer waistband. Repeat with the remaining front and back waistbands; this piece will now be referred to as the inner waistband.

11. With right sides together, place the outer waistband along the bottom edge of the bodice, ensuring that the notches match: align the single notches on the front waistband with the front bodice waist darts. The seam between the front and back waistband pieces should align with the right-hand side seam of the bodice. Pin in place. Place the inner waistband right side down on the wrong side of the bodice, again matching the notches and side seams; the inner and outer waistbands should sandwich the bodice at the waistline. Pin in place and sew through all layers.

12. With the seam allowance facing the inner waistband, understitch (see page 35) the seam allowances to the inner waistband to ensure that the waistband stays in place. The stitches should not be visible on the right side of your pinafore.

15 – Topstitch

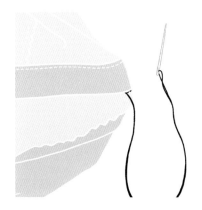

15 – Slipstitch

13. At this point there will be too much bulk inside your waistband, so trim the seam allowance down to 6mm (¼in) and press the waistband down.

14. The inner waistband now needs to be pushed up out of the way. With right sides together, pin the skirt to the bottom edge of the outer waistband. Note that the notches have to match: match the double notches on the back waistband to the double notches at the top edge of the back skirt, and the single notches on the front waistband to the single notches at the top edge of the front skirt. Stitch the outer waistband to the skirt, trim the seam allowance and press the seam allowance up towards the bodice.

15. Fold under 1cm (⅜in) along the bottom edge of the inner waistband and press. Pin this folded edge to the waistline, over the seam allowance from the previous step, and sew the inner waistband in place. If you sew this step with a machine, the stitches will be visible on the outside of the garment, so if you wish, you can make this a design feature by also topstitching around the top edge of the waistband from the right side. Alternatively, slipstitch the folded edge to the inside of the skirt by hand; these stitches will barely be visible on the outside.

16. The left-hand side seam of the skirt and waistband have not yet been stitched; insert the zip here (see *Essential skill: Inserting a centred zip*, overleaf).

Project continues overleaf

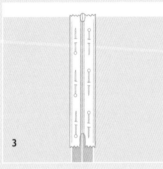

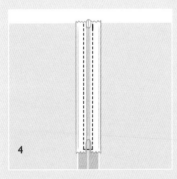

Tip:
At Step 4, the zip pull might get
in the way of sewing straight
stitches. If so, unpick a few
basting stitches and move the
pull out of the way.

Essential skill

INSERTING A CENTRED ZIP

Centred zips are also known as regular zips; they are the most
common zips found in shop-bought clothes. I have a very simple
technique for inserting them, for which you will need a zip foot.

1. With the raw edges of your fabric finished, mark the zip
   notch; this is where the end of your zip will be.

2. With right sides together, sew basting stitches (your longest
   sewing machine stitch) from the top edge of the garment
   to the zip notch you made in step 1. Backstitch at the zip
   notch. Switch your sewing machine back to its regular
   stitch length. Sew from the zip notch to the end of the
   seam. Press the seam allowance open.

3. Place the zip face down on the wrong side of your garment
   and pin it in place. The bottom stop of the zip should be
   above the backstitching you did in step 2. The zip coil
   should also be in line with the centre of the seam. If you
   wish, you can also tack the zip in place by hand.

4. Change over to your machine's zip foot and sew down one
   side of the zip to the bottom stop. With the needle down,
   raise the presser foot and pivot to sew across the base of the
   zip. Stop and pivot again. Sew to the top of the zipper and
   backstitch.

5. Using a seam ripper, unpick the basting stitches from
   step 2 above, stopping at the zip notch backstitching.
   Press the seam.

FINISHING TOUCHES

17. Continuing from your backstitches from step 7, above, now sew in the bias tape that you left unstitched before.

18. Trim the seam allowance down to 3mm (⅛in), fold over the bias tape to the wrong side of the pinafore and press in place. Repeat step 17 at the other side of the zip.

19. Sew as close as possible to the bias tape fold, but be careful as you get nearer to the zip coil. Backstitch just before you get to the zip coil.

20. Hand sew the small hook-and-eye closure onto the top of the left side seam for added security. Sew the hook onto the right side and the eye onto the left side to correspond.

21. Finish the raw edges around the hem of the skirt and fold the bottom edge over to the wrong side by 1cm (⅜in). Press, pin and stitch in place. Give your pinafore a final steam press.

Variations

- Ditch the front bodice and the back panels to transform the project into a circular skirt. For this, you will need to use a shorter zip, of around 18cm (7in).

- Add a rectangular pair of patch pockets (see page 152).

- Use contrasting fabrics for the skirt and bodice for a statement look.

Jade couture dress

YOU WILL NEED

Light- to medium-weight woven
  fabric of your choice (for amount,
  see below)
50cm (20in) very lightweight iron-on
  (fusible) interfacing
1m (1yd) elastic, 1cm (⅜in) wide
55cm (22in) lightweight invisible zip
Small hook-and-eye closure
Matching sewing machine thread
Basic sewing kit (see page 10)
Invisible zip foot

This elegant dress combines several of the essential skills we've already
covered (a gathered three-tier skirt, a neckline facing and inserting sleeves),
but takes things up a notch by gathering the sleeve heads and elasticating
the cuffs to create dramatic statement sleeves. It also features an invisible
zip in the back bodice – a technique that gives fitted dresses an impressive
couture-style finish.

GARMENT SIZE	6	8	10	12	14	16	18	20	22	24	26	28
FABRIC QUANTITY (M)	2.54	2.55	2.56	2.63	2.67	2.74	2.76	2.78	2.89	3.11	3.24	3.4
FABRIC QUANTITY (YD)	2¾	2¾	2⅞	2⅞	3	3	3	3⅛	3¼	3½	3⅝	3¾

FABRIC SUGGESTIONS
Pick fabrics with some softness and
drape, such as lightweight cotton,
viscose/rayon, gingham, chambray,
crepe, voile, georgette or soft
lightweight linen. A simple block
colour or bold print could work well,
as could a small-scale print or polka
dots, stripes or geometric prints.

PATTERN INVENTORY

1. **Front bodice** cut 1 on the fold from fabric

2. **Back bodice** cut 1 pair from fabric

3. **Sleeve** cut 1 pair from fabric

4. **Front top skirt** cut 1 on the fold from fabric

5. **Back top skirt** cut 1 pair from fabric

6. **Cuff** cut 1 pair from fabric

7. **Front and back mid skirt** cut 2 on the fold from fabric

8. **Front and back lower skirt** cut 2 on the fold from fabric

9. **Back neck facing** cut 1 pair from fabric and 1 pair from
   interfacing

10. **Front neck facing** cut 1 on the fold from fabric and 1 on
    the fold from interfacing

Project continues overleaf

FABRIC CUTTING LAYOUT

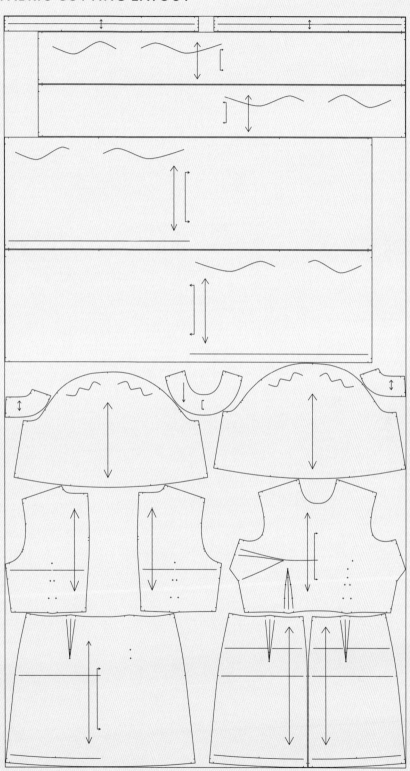

Note:
Sample cutting layout for size 18 on 150cm (60in) fabric width on the fold.

3 – Front

3 – Back

PREPARE YOUR FABRIC

1. Prepare and press your fabric (see page 19). Cut out the pieces, transferring all pattern markings to the fabric (see page 33). Following the manufacturer's instructions, apply interfacing to the wrong side of the front and back neck facings.

2. Staystitch (see page 35) around the front and back bodice necklines and the top curved edge of the facings to prevent the neckline from stretching out of shape.

ASSEMBLE THE BODICE

3. Fold, pin and sew the bust and waist darts on the front and back bodices (see page 39). Press the bust darts (on the front bodice) down towards the waist and the waist darts (on the front and back bodices) towards the side seams. Allow to cool.

4. With right sides together, pin and sew the front and back bodices together at the shoulders. Finish the raw edges (see page 40). Press the shoulder seams open.

INSERT THE SLEEVES

On the sleeve pattern, wavy lines indicate where to gather the sleeves.

5. Sew two lines of gathering stitches where the sleeves need to be gathered (see *Essential skill: Sewing gathers*, page 63) within the seam allowance, from one notch to the other.

6. Lay the bodice out flat. With right sides together, pin the sleeves into the bodice, ensuring that the front and back notches match. Adjust the gathers until they fit within the notch markings on the armholes.

Tip:
A double notch indicates the back of the sleeve and a single notch indicates the front. Match these notches to the corresponding notches on the front and back bodices.

7. With the sleeve on top so that you can control the gathers, sew the sleeves in place. Finish the raw edges of the sleeve seam allowance (see page 40). Press the seam allowances towards the bodice.

FINISH THE BODICE

8. With right sides together, pin the front and back bodices together at the side and underarm seams, ensuring that the armhole seams match. Starting at the waistline, sew the side and underarm seam on each side in one continuous line of stitching. Finish the raw edges of the side seam allowances and press the seams open.

ATTACH THE CUFFS AND ELASTIC TO THE SLEEVES

9. With right sides together, pin and sew the short edges of each cuff together to form a wide tube. Press the seam allowances open. Fold the cuff in half lengthways, with wrong sides together, and press.

10. With right sides together, aligning the raw edges of the cuffs and the sleeve ends, pin the cuffs over the sleeve ends. Sew in place, leaving an 8-cm (3-in) gap at the underarm seam for the elastic.

Project continues overleaf

PROJECTS

<u>How much elastic?</u>

To work out how much elastic you need, measure around your upper arm, then subtract 5–10cm (2–4in) from this measurement, depending on how snugly you want it to fit around your arm.

11. Cut two pieces of elastic to the required length (see above), then attach one end of each piece to a safety pin or bodkin. Slide it through the gap in the cuff. Overlap the ends of the elastic by about 1.5cm (⅝in) and pin them together. Change your sewing machine to the zig-zag stitch function and stitch over the ends of the elastic, going back and forth three or four times to ensure the elastic is secure.

12. Switch back to a regular straight stitch and stitch the gap you left for the elastic closed. Finish the seam allowances and press towards the cuffs.

MAKE UP THE TOP SKIRT

13. Fold, pin and sew the skirt waist darts in the front and back top skirts (see steps 3 and 4).

14. With right sides together, matching the notches, pin and sew the front and back skirts together at the side seams. Finish the raw edges on the side seams and the bottom edge of the skirt and press the seams open. Do not sew the centre back seam of the back skirt, as this is where the zip will be inserted.

Project continues overleaf

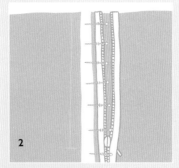

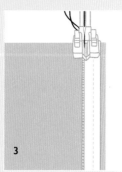

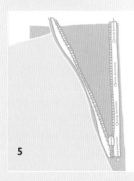

INSERTING AN INVISIBLE ZIP

Invisible zips are sewn to the seam allowance to keep them hidden inside garments. They are sewn using an invisible zip foot, which has grooves that hold and guide the zip teeth in place while the zip tape is being stitched.

1. Starting at the neckline, draw the seamline all the way down both centre back pieces. This is where the zip teeth will sit when the zip is inserted. Measure and mark where the zip teeth should end.

2. Attach an invisible zip foot to your machine and undo the zip. Place the zip face down on the right side of the garment, aligning the zip teeth with the drawn line. Pin the zip tape in place. If you wish, you can hand or machine baste the zip tape, too.

3. Slot the zip teeth into the right-hand groove of the invisible zip foot. Starting from the top of the zip, sew all the way down the zip tape, backstitching at the end.

4. Before you sew the other side of the zip, check that the zip can close properly. If it doesn't, unpick the stitches and sew them again.

5. Pin the other side of the zip to the other garment piece, again with the zip teeth running along the drawn line. Pin, hand or machine baste in place if you wish, then stitch as before.

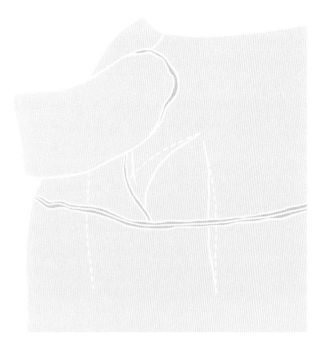

15

ATTACH THE TOP SKIRT TO THE BODICE

15. With right sides together, matching the side seams and darts, pin the bodice over the top skirt, temporarily pinning or tacking the centre back of the skirt at the waistline to hold everything in place while you sew. Sew along the waistline. Finish the raw edges of the waistline seam allowance and press the seam allowance down towards the hem of the skirt.

INSERT THE INVISIBLE ZIP

16. Finish the raw edges from the back neckline to the hem of the top skirt. Insert the invisible zip (see *Essential skill: Inserting an invisible zip*, opposite).

17. Pin the rest of the centre back seam right sides together. Change the invisible zip foot to a regular foot. Starting from the bottom edge of the skirt, sew the top skirt centre back seam, stopping right at the end of the invisible zip stitches. Press the seam allowance open.

Project continues overleaf

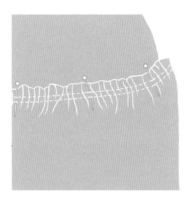

21 – detail

21

SEW THE MID AND LOWER SKIRTS

This dress features exposed gathers, which are stitched on top of the top and mid skirt panels. This means that the top edges of the mid and lower skirt panels have to be folded twice and pressed to conceal the raw edges of the fabric.

18. With right sides together, pin and sew the side seams of the mid skirt, finish the raw edges and press flat. Repeat with the lower skirt.

19. At the top edges of the mid and lower skirts, fold 1cm (⅜in) to the wrong side and press. Now fold 1.5cm (⅝in) to the wrong side, press and sew 1.2cm (½in) from the edge of the fabric.

20. Sew two rows of gathering stitches (see *Essential skill: Sewing gathers*, page 63) along the top edge of the mid skirt. The gathering stitches should be below the top edge hems. Gently pull the top bobbin threads to gather the top edge of the mid skirt, making sure that the gathers are evenly distributed all the way around. Finish the raw edge of the bottom of the mid skirt (see page 40) . Repeat with the lower skirt.

ATTACH THE MID AND LOWER SKIRTS TO THE DRESS

21. Aligning the side seams and notches, pin the gathered edge of the lower skirt on top of the bottom edge of the mid skirt (the *wrong* side of the lower skirt should be on top of the *right* side of the mid skirt). Sew in between the rows of gathering stitches, with the gathers facing you. Carefully remove the gathering threads. Attach the mid skirt to the top half of the dress in the same way.

Project continues overleaf

ATTACH THE NECKLINE FACING

22. With right sides together, pin and sew the front and back facings together at the shoulders. Press the seam allowances open. Finish the raw outer edge.

23. With right sides together and shoulder seams matching, place the facing around the neckline of the bodice and pin all the way to the invisible zip tape; make sure the invisible zip tape is lying flat and the centre back seam allowance is facing upwards. Sew the facing in place using a 1cm (⅜in) seam allowance. Trim the seam allowance and notch the corners and curves (see page 38). Stabilize the facing by attaching it to the bodice shoulder seam allowance either by machine sewing into the shoulder seam or by hand stitching it to the bodice seam allowance.

24. Turn the facing to the wrong side and gently press out the corners. Starting from the centre back, understitch around the neckline (see page 35), using your presser foot width as a guide to stitch as close as possible to the neckline seam.

FINISH THE NECKLINE

Tip:
Note that the stitching should only go through the facing, the dress centre back seam allowance and the zip tape.

25. With the dress right side up and the facing wrong side up, align the raw edge of the facing and the finished centre back edge of the dress. Fold the neckline seam allowance down. Pin in place, catching the zip tape. Sew as close as possible to the invisible zip teeth (roughly 3mm/⅛in from the groove of the zip teeth beneath the facing). Sew down to the end of the facing and backstitch.

26. Carefully trim the top corner of the seam allowance, avoiding the stitches and the zip. Tuck the raw edges into the wrong side and use a blunt-tipped object such as a chopstick or knitting needle to poke out the corner. There should be no visible stitches on the main garment.

25

27. Hand stitch the small hook-and eye-closure onto the top of the facing for added security. Sew the hook onto the right side and the eye onto the left side to correspond.

HEM THE DRESS

28. Around the bottom edge, press under a double 1cm (⅜in) hem to the wrong side of the dress. Pin and sew the hem, backstitching at the end of the hem. Press the dress.

Variation

Sew two rows of gathering stitches along the bottom edge of mid skirt. Lightly gather the bottom edge of mid skirt before attaching the lower skirt panel for a bubble effect.

Jasmine duster

YOU WILL NEED

Light- to medium-weight woven
   fabric of your choice (for amount,
   see below)
Matching sewing machine thread
Basic sewing kit (see page 10)

With 'grown-on' sleeves (sleeves that are part of the front and back pattern pieces and therefore do not need to be inserted separately), no tricky closures such as zips or buttonholes and an easy-to-attach centre front band that also covers the back neckline, this project is the perfect way to boost your confidence in sewing. More relaxed than a dressy jacket but smarter than a cardigan, it can be made using bold prints, or block colours for understated elegance.

GARMENT SIZE	6	8	10	12	14	16	18	20	22	24	26	28
FABRIC QUANTITY (M)	2.09	2.13	2.14	2.15	2.17	2.18	2.2	2.52	2.64	2.67	2.7	2.7
FABRIC QUANTITY (YD)	$2\frac{1}{3}$	$2\frac{1}{3}$	$2\frac{1}{3}$	$2\frac{1}{3}$	$2\frac{1}{3}$	$2\frac{1}{2}$	$2\frac{1}{2}$	$2\frac{3}{4}$	3	3	3	3

FABRIC SUGGESTIONS
Look for fabrics with a relaxed drape, such as viscose/rayon, georgette or soft cotton. For a more structured feel, densely woven cotton blends, jacquard or lightweight denim are ideal.

PATTERN INVENTORY

1. **Front** cut 1 one pair

2. **Back** cut 1 on the fold

3. **Neckband** cut 2 pairs

Project continues overleaf

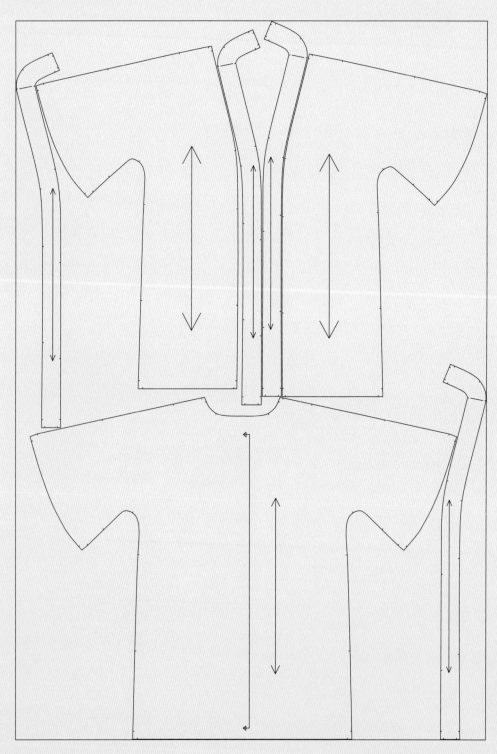

Note:
Sample cutting layout for size 18 on 150cm (60in) fabric width on the fold.

JASMINE DUSTER

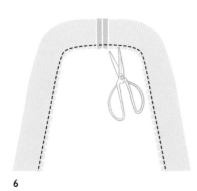

6

PREPARE YOUR FABRIC

1. Prepare and press your fabric (see page 19). Cut out the pieces, transferring all pattern markings to the fabric (see page 33).

2. Staystitch (see page 35) around the back neckline to stop the fabric from stretching out of shape.

ASSEMBLE THE FRONT AND BACK

3. With right sides together, matching the notches, pin and sew the front to the back at the shoulder seams. Finish the raw edges and press the seams open.

4. With right sides together, pin and sew the side seams, being careful to maintain the seam allowance while sewing along the curved underarm area. Clip into the underarm seam allowance (see page 38), avoiding the stitches. Finish the raw edges of the side seams. Press the seams open.

SEW THE NECKBAND

5. With right sides together, pin one pair of neckbands together at the centre back (marked CB) and sew. Press the seam open; there's no need to finish raw edges at this point. Repeat with the second pair of neckbands. You now have two long neckbands, each with a seam at the centre back.

6. With right sides together, matching the CB seams and notches, pin and sew the two long neckbands together along the inner seam line. Clip into the seam allowance (see page 38) and press the seam allowance towards the neckband.

7. Understitch (see page 35) the seam allowances onto one neckband. The understitching will enable the internal neckband to stay in place and remain invisible.

Project continues overleaf

8. Fold the neckband so that the wrong sides are together and press carefully.

9. With right sides together, matching the notches and raw edges, pin the neckband to the opening of the front of the duster, making sure the understitched side is underneath; the notch marked SS on the neckband should match the shoulder seam on the duster. Sew from one end of the duster to the other, being careful to maintain the width of the seam allowance when sewing around the curved neckline.

10. Finish the raw edge on the seam allowance and press the seam allowance towards the duster.

HEM AND FINISH

11. At the bottom edge of the duster, finish the raw edge. Fold over and press 2.5cm (1in) to the wrong side, pin and sew close to the edge.

12. Finish the raw edge of the sleeves. Fold over and press 1.5cm (⅝in) to the wrong side, pin and sew close to the edge. Give your duster a final steam press.

Variation

Try lengthening or shortening the duster for a different look.

Josie princess seam dress

Now for a garment that's a little more fitted than the ones earlier in this book. This dress has a classic shift silhouette, with princess seams that are fitted through the bust and stretch all the way to the hem to elongate the body, and it also features handy in-seam pockets. Although it might look a little daunting at first sight, you've handled many of the techniques (neckline facings, inserting sleeves and invisible zips) already, so you're simply building on what you've already learnt. Just take your time and concentrate on keeping your seam allowances a consistent width – particularly on the princess seams that run down the front.

YOU WILL NEED
Medium-weight woven fabric of your choice (for amount, see below)
50cm (20in) very lightweight iron-on (fusible) interfacing
Matching sewing machine thread
55cm (22in) invisible zip
Small hook-and-eye closure
Basic sewing kit (see page 10)
Invisible zip foot

GARMENT SIZE	6	8	10	12	14	16	18	20	22	24	26	28
FABRIC QUANTITY (M)	1.56	1.57	1.59	1.72	1.75	1.83	1.9	1.94	2.04	2.16	2.27	2.32
FABRIC QUANTITY (YD)	1¾	1¾	1¾	2	2	2	2⅛	2⅛	2¼	2⅜	2½	2⅝

FABRIC SUGGESTIONS
Select medium-weight woven fabrics to give your dress the intended structure and shape, such as lightweight denim, cotton sateen, lightweight wool, jacquard, crepe or chambray. Stay away from lightweight, stretchy or drapey fabrics.

PATTERN INVENTORY

1. **Centre front** cut 1 on the fold from fabric

2. **Upper side** front cut 1 pair from fabric

3. **Lower side** front cut 1 pair from fabric

4. **Centre back** cut 1 pair from fabric

5. **Side back** cut 1 pair from fabric

6. **Pocket bag** cut 1 pair from fabric

7. **Sleeve** cut 1 pair from fabric

8. **Back neck facing** cut 1 pair from fabric and 1 pair from interfacing

9. **Front neck facing** cut 1 on the fold from fabric and 1 on the fold from interfacing

Project continues overleaf

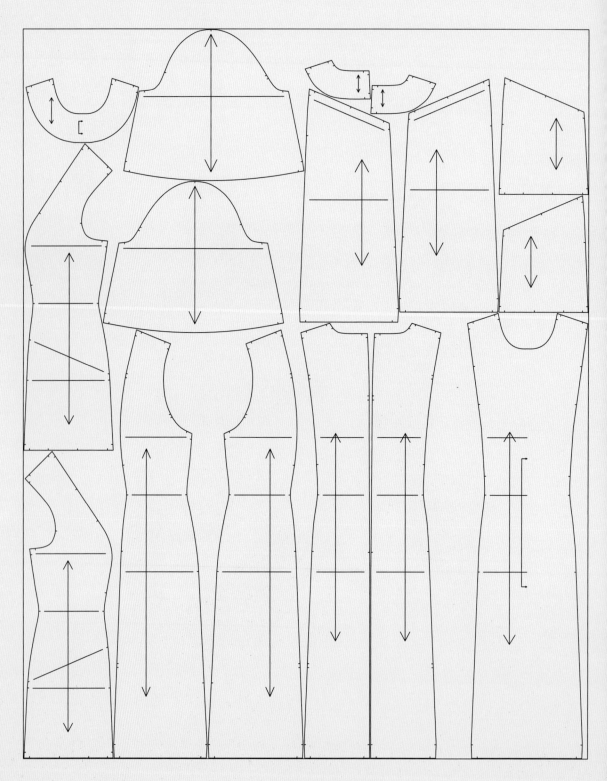

PREPARE YOUR FABRIC

1. Prepare and press your fabric (see page 19). Cut out the pieces, transferring all pattern markings to the fabric (see page 33). Following the manufacturer's instructions, apply interfacing to the wrong side of the front and back neck facing pieces.

2. Staystitch (see page 35) around the neckline of the following pieces: centre front, centre back, back neck facing and front neck facing.

3

INSERT THE IN-SEAM POCKETS

3. With right sides together, matching the notches, pin and sew the pocket bag to the top edge of the lower side front. Press the seam allowances towards the pocket bag and understitch the seam allowances to the pocket bag.

4. Fold the pocket over to the wrong side of the lower side front and press. Topstitch 7mm (¼in) from the edge. Repeat steps 3 and 4 on the other side with the remaining pocket bag and lower side front.

Project continues overleaf

Note:
Sample cutting
layout for size 18 on
150cm (60in) fabric
width on the fold.

PROJECTS

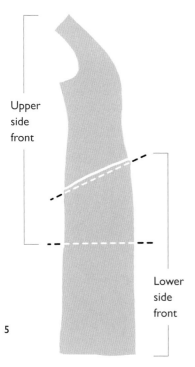

Upper
side
front

Lower
side
front

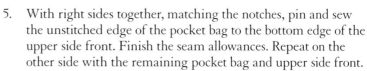

5

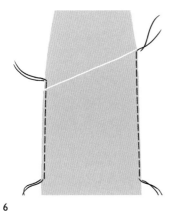

6

8

5. With right sides together, matching the notches, pin and sew the unstitched edge of the pocket bag to the bottom edge of the upper side front. Finish the seam allowances. Repeat on the other side with the remaining pocket bag and upper side front.

6. Matching the notches, baste the upper and lower side front pieces together along the pocket bag sides to keep the pocket in place.

SEW THE FRONT AND BACK PRINCESS SEAMS

7. Finish the raw side edges of the centre and side pieces.

8. With right sides together, matching the notches, pin and sew one side piece to each side of the centre front panel. To reduce bulk and improve the tension in the seam, snip into the seam allowance along the bust curve (taking care not to cut into any stitches) and press the seam allowance open. Stitch the side back pieces to the centre back pieces in the same way, without stitching the centre back seam.

9. Pin and sew the front and back pieces together at the shoulders. Finish the seam allowances and press the seams open.

Project continues overleaf

SEW THE SLEEVES

10. With right sides together, pin the sleeves into the armholes of the dress, making sure the sleeve notches match the armhole notches (double notches on the back of the sleeves and armholes, single notches on the front of the sleeves and armholes, and the midpoint notches on the sleeves matching the shoulder seams). Sew the sleeves to the armholes, finish the raw edges and press the seam allowances towards the dress.

FINISH THE SIDE SEAMS AND CENTRE BACK

11. With right sides together, pin the dress front and back together at the side seams. Sew from the hem of the sleeves, pivot at the underarm seam and sew to the hem of the dress. Finish the side seam raw edges and press the seam open. Remove the basting stitches that were holding the pocket bags in place.

12. Finish the raw edges along the two centre back pieces.

13. Insert the invisible zip in the centre back opening (see *Essential skill: Inserting an invisible zip*, page 94). Do take the time to match the top edge of the zipper tapes with the raw edge of the back neckline.

14. Pin the rest of the centre back seam right sides together. Change the invisible zip foot back to a regular foot. Starting from the bottom edge of the dress, sew the rest of the centre back seam, stopping right at the end of the invisible zip stitches. Press the seam allowance open.

Project continues overleaf

ATTACH THE NECKLINE FACING

15. With right sides together, pin and sew the front and back facings together at the shoulders. Press the seam allowances open. Finish the raw bottom outer edge of the facing.

16. With right sides together and the invisible zip open, matching the shoulder seams, pin the facing around the neckline of the dress, pinning it over the invisible zip tape; make sure the invisible zip tape is lying flat and the centre back seam allowance under the zip is opened out and facing upwards. Sew the facing in place with a 1cm (⅜in) seam allowance. Trim the seam allowance and clip into the seam allowance at the curves.

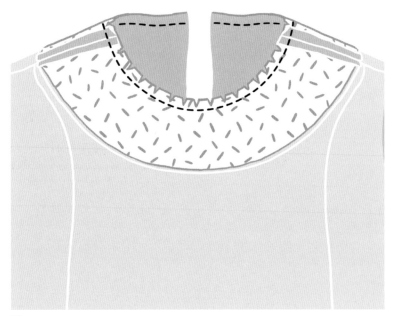

16

FINISH THE NECKLINE

17. Starting from the centre back, understitch the facing around the neckline (see page 35), stitching only through the facing and seam allowances and using your presser foot width as a guide to stitch as close as possible to the curved edge. Bear in mind that the understitching should not be visible on the right side of the dress.

18. With the dress right side up and the facing wrong side up, align the raw edge of the facing and the finished centre back edges of the dress, then pin the side edges of the facing in place, catching the zip tape. Sewing as close as possible to the invisible zip teeth (roughly 3mm/⅛in from the groove of the zip teeth beneath the facing), sew down to the end of the facing and backstitch. Carefully trim off the top corner of the seam allowance, avoiding the stitches and the zip.

19. Turn the facing to the wrong side and use a blunt-tipped object such as a chopstick or knitting needle to poke out the corners. There should be no visible stitches on the right side of the garment.

20. Hand sew the small hook-and-eye closure onto the top of the facing for added security. Sew the hook onto the right side and the eye onto the left side to correspond.

HEM THE DRESS AND SLEEVES

21. Around the hem, fold 1cm (⅜in) and then 2.5cm (1in) to the wrong side and press. Stitch close to the fold. Hem the sleeves with a 1.5cm (⅝in) single hem.

Juliette wrap dress

YOU WILL NEED

Light- to medium-weight woven
   fabric of your choice (for amount,
   see below)
4m (4yd) coordinating double-fold
   13mm (½in) bias binding
Matching sewing machine thread
Contrasting sewing machine thread
   for gathering stitches
Basic sewing kit (see page 10)
Loop turner, knitting needle or any
   simple turning tool

A wrap dress is a classic, flattering design that looks far more difficult to sew than it actually is. This one has 'grown-on' sleeves (sleeves that are cut as part of the front and back bodice sections, rather than attached separately) and the wrap-around skirt is fastened with hassle-free ties rather than fiddly zips or buttonholes. Dress it up with heeled sandals and a minimalist bag for an elevated day look and add a few jewels for the evening.

GARMENT SIZE	6	8	10	12	14	16	18	20	22	24	26	28
FABRIC QUANTITY (M)	2.24	2.27	2.29	2.35	2.42	2.45	2.54	2.6	2.64	2.69	2.72	2.74
FABRIC QUANTITY (YD)	2½	2½	2½	2⅝	2⅔	2¾	2⅞	2⅞	3	3	3	3

FABRIC SUGGESTIONS

Opt for fabrics with some softness and drape, such as lightweight cotton, viscose/rayon, gingham, chambray, crepe, voile, georgette or soft lightweight linen. Fabrics with all-over prints, such as Ankara (African wax print) fabrics, would also be great for this design: because of the absence of darts and set-in sleeves, very little pattern matching is required.

PATTERN INVENTORY

1. **Front bodice** cut 2

2. **Back bodice** cut 1 on the fold

3. **Left front skirt** cut 1

4. **Right front skirt** cut 1

5. **Back skirt** cut 1 on the fold

6. **Left tie** cut 1

7. **Right tie** cut 1

Project continues overleaf

FABRIC CUTTING LAYOUT

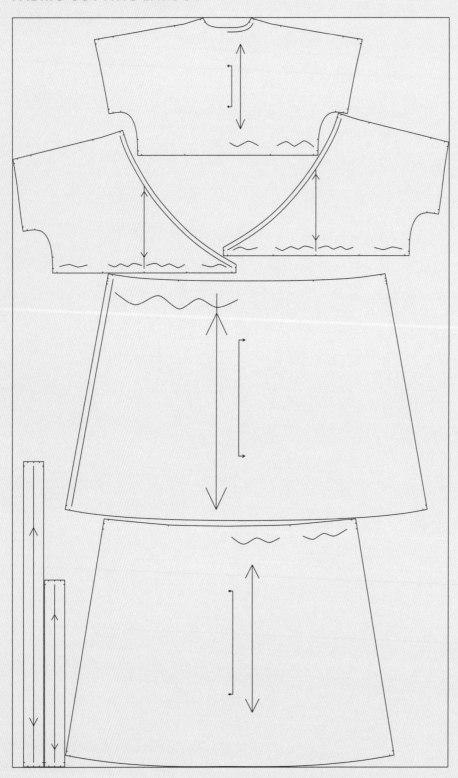

PREPARE YOUR FABRIC

1. Prepare and press your fabric (see page 19). Cut out the pieces, transferring all pattern markings to the fabric (see page 33).

2. Staystitch (see page 35) around the necklines of the front and back bodices, stitching within 1cm (⅜in) of the seam allowance. (Wrap bodice necklines are known to stretch out of shape and look unattractive if not given special preparation before all the sewing.)

3. Make the open-ended ties (see *Essential skill: Waist ties and sashes,* overleaf).

6

SEW THE BODICE

4. Finish the raw edges of the front and back bodice pieces (see page 40), except for the waistline and the staystitched front and back necklines.

5. With right sides together, lay the front bodice pieces on top of the back bodice. Pin and then sew the shoulder seams. Press the shoulder seams open.

6. Fold the front and back bodices at the shoulders, so that they're right sides together. Mark the position of the notches for the waist tie opening on the right-hand bodice pieces.

7. On the right-hand side, sew from the end of the sleeve down to the first notch, which is close to the waistline, then backstitch. Cut the threads and position your needle exactly at the second notch. Sew those few stitches to the waistline, then backstitch. Sew the left-hand side underarm and side seam without any openings.

8. Press open the seam allowances and sew a rectangle around the opening for the waist ties to secure the seam allowance in place.

8

Note:
Sample cutting
layout for size 18 on
150cm (60in) fabric
width on the fold.

Project continues overleaf

Essential skill

WAIST TIES AND SASHES

Ties are used in a range of ways in different garments, and always
need to be turned right side out. There are many loop-turning
tools on the market, but I have also seen unconventional items
such as knitting needles, pens, tweezers, hair clips, chopsticks and
threads used for loop turning.

The Juliette dress has two waist ties that have one raw edge, but
you may also want to learn to create waist ties or waist sashes that
have both ends neatly sewn. I will show how to create both types.

Open-ended ties (used in this project)

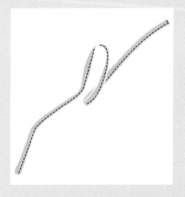 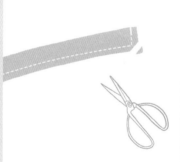 

Step 1: Fold the tie in half
widthways, with right sides
together, pin and press. Sew
across one short end. When
you get to the corner, pivot
and sew along the long raw
edges. Backstitch at the end
of the tie, leaving the second
short end open.

Step 2: Trim the corner from
the sewn right angle, avoiding
cutting into the stitches, to get a
clean, sharp angle when the ties
are turned inside out. Trim all
around the seam allowance.

Step 3: Using a loop turner, a
blunt-tipped chopstick or even
a chunky knitting needle,
push the fabric through the
tube until you've turned the
tie right side out. Press well.

Tip:
In order to know where exactly
you should pivot and turn a corner,
measure and lightly mark the pivot
spots with a sharp chalk pencil.

Closed ties

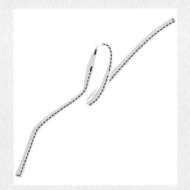 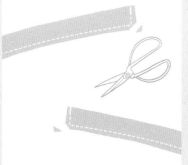 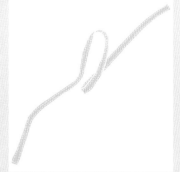

Step 1: Fold the tie in half widthways, with right sides together, and pin in place. Sew across one short end, pivot at the corner and sew to the middle of the tie. Backstitch and cut off the threads. Leave an 8cm (3in) gap, then continue sewing to the other end, again pivoting at the corner to form a neat right angle.

Step 2: Trim the corners from the sewn right angles, and trim the rest of the seam allowance.

Step 3: Turn the tie right side out through the gap and press carefully. Topstitch (see page 35) around the tie; this will also close the gap in the middle of the long edge.

9. Fold the ends of the sleeves over to the wrong side by 1.5cm (⅝in), press and pin in place. Sew the sleeve hems close to the finished ends.

10. The bodice of the dress has no darts and all the shaping is done by subtle gathers around the waistline. Measure your waist to get a rough idea of how long the bodice waistline will be. At this stage, you can customize the waistline to your desired fit – it can be as loose or as fitted as you wish. Add a 2cm (¾in) seam allowance to the measurement and record the figure for the next step.

Tip:
I recommend using contrasting threads at this point because a few steps down the line, there will be a lot of gathering threads and it's easy to confuse them with the waistline stitches.

11. At the bottom edge (the waistline) of the bodice, starting and ending 8cm (3in) away from the side seams, sew two parallel rows of gathering stitches (see *Essential skill: Sewing gathers*, page 63) on both the front and the back. Gather the bodice to the measurement you recorded in step 10, distributing the gathers evenly.

SEW THE FRONT AND BACK SKIRTS

12. With right sides together, pin and sew the front skirts to the back skirt at the side seams. Finish the raw edges and press the side seams open. Don't join the panels into a loop – leave the front edges unstitched for the wrap-around section.

Project continues overleaf

17

13. Sew two rows of gathering stitches at the top edge of the skirt, again starting and ending 8cm (3in) from the raw edges. Gather the skirt to the measurement you recorded in step 10, distributing the gathers evenly. Carefully pull the top bobbin threads to create evenly distributed gathers that match the waistline figure you recorded above. The bodice and skirt waistlines should now match in length.

JOIN THE SKIRT AND THE BODICE AT THE WAISTLINE

14. With right sides together and the gathers evenly distributed, matching the side seams and notches, pin the bodice and skirt together. Sew them together, gently easing the gathers through your sewing machine. Backstitch at the start and end of this long waist seam.

15. Carefully unpick the gathering stitches, being careful not to unpick the actual waistline stitches. At this point, you will reap the benefits of having used contrasting threads for the gathering stitches.

16. Finish the waistline seam allowance and press it upwards.

SECURE THE WAIST TIES

Note that the waist ties are different lengths – the left tie has to match the left skirt and the right tie matches the right skirt.

17. Locate the 'waist tie' notches at the top edge of your left and right front skirts and pin the raw edge of your waist ties to the right sides of the fabric. Using long basting stitches, secure the waist ties in place.

BIND THE RAW EDGES

You will need enough bias binding to finish off the raw edges around the bodice and the wrap-over skirt sections.

18. Unfold the bias binding along one long edge. Starting from the hem of the left front skirt, pin this edge around the unfinished edges of the dress, right sides together. Gently ease the tape around the waistline seam, ensuring that the waist ties are out of the way, and then pin it all the way to the raw edge of the right front skirt hem. Trim any excess bias tape.

19. Using a 1cm (⅜in) seam allowance, following the first fold of the bias tape, stitch the binding in place.

20. Understitch (see page 35) the newly sewn seam allowance onto the bias tape on the other side. This is to keep the bias tape in its place on the wrong side of your dress and prevent it from showing on the right side.

21. Fold the bias tape over to the wrong side and pin it in place. Topstitch the seam allowance in place and press.

HEM THE DRESS

22. Finish the raw edge of the dress hem. Fold over and press 1.5cm (⅝in) to the wrong side and pin in place. Topstitch the hem and give the dress a final steam press.

Upcycling projects

Once you make the decision to change the way you look at items of clothing, you will begin to see that the possibilities for creation and re-creation are endless. These potential changes could range from adding or removing elements from a garment all the way to chopping up an old item of clothing to transform it into something completely new.

This process is known as upcycling, and it involves working with a piece of clothing and giving it a new lease of life, usually while maintaining some core elements of the original item. Whether it is your former bedding, old curtains, over- or undersized clothes, an old leather sofa, wedding dress or vintage garments from a charity shop, you can always upcycle and repurpose to give the piece added value and an extended life.

Perhaps you have a dress in your wardrobe that you've fallen out of love with or that no longer goes with your look. Transform the way you feel about it by adding a new detail: you could embellish the collar or change up the buttons. Or maybe you have a beloved piece of clothing that no longer fits you. Before you think about giving it away, why not grab a pair of scissors and have a go at converting it into something new to treasure?

The projects in this section range from transforming old pieces of clothing into new wardrobe staples to turning scrap pieces of fabric into stunning new creations.

Oversized shirt to gathered skirt

Old, oversized men's shirts can be very simply upcycled by sewing along the side seams to make them fit better or by shortening the sleeves. But why not try a more adventurous transformation by chopping off the top section to create your own unique, gathered skirt?

YOU WILL NEED
Oversized man's shirt
Matching sewing machine thread
Elastic, 2.5cm (1in) wide
Basic sewing kit (see page 10)
Safety pin or bodkin

NOTE
A 1.5cm (⅝in) seam allowance is used throughout unless otherwise specified. For a clean, professional look, finish the raw edges of the fabric as you work (see page 40), using your preferred method.

1. Start by steam pressing the shirt to remove any kinks and creases. Next, cut off the sleeves by following the sleeve stitch line along the armhole.

2. Using a ruler and tailor's chalk, draw a straight line beneath the shirt collar stand, running just below the top panel of the back piece (called the 'yoke'). Cut away the top section of the shirt along your drawn line.

3. Depending on the design of the shirt, unpick any pleats at the back of the shirt. Using a steam iron, press away any pleat creases.

4. From the top edge of the shirt, draw a diagonal line down to the side seam at an angle of about 30 degrees. Cut along the line.

Project continues overleaf

2

4

UPCYCLING PROJECTS

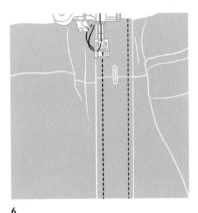

6

5.   Turn the shirt inside out and pin the new side seams. Sew the side seams and finish the raw edges. Press the seams open.

6.   Turn the shirt right side out again. Remove the top button to allow for stitching the elastic casing. Make sure all the other buttons are fastened, then sew both sides of the button band, following the original stitch lines.

7.   To create the elastic casing around the waist, fold over and press the top edge of the shirt to the wrong side by 1cm (⅜in) and then again by 3cm (1¼in). Press and pin in place. Sew as close as you can to the folded edge, leaving an 8cm (3in) gap for the elastic to be passed through the casing.

8.   Cut a piece of elastic to the length you require (see *How much elastic should I cut?*, page 61). Attach a safety pin or bodkin to one end. Insert the safety pin or bodkin into the gap and feed it around the channel, taking care not to twist the elastic as you do so. Once the safety pin or bodkin has gone all around the casing, overlap the ends of the elastic and pin them together. Switch your sewing machine setting to a zig-zag stitch, then sew back and forth over the elastic ends a few times to secure them in place.

9.   Switch your machine back to a regular straight stitch. Pin and sew the gap in your waist channel, following the stitch line from step 7. Finally, sew the button that you removed in step 6 back in its original position.

Add flutter sleeves to a dress or top

YOU WILL NEED

Sleeveless dress or top
Wide, lighter-weight fabric
recovered from old clothes or soft
furnishings. To get the right
amount, work out how long you
want the sleeve to be, add 3cm
(1¼in) for seam allowances and
hems, and cut two squares to this
measurement.
Matching sewing machine thread
Basic sewing kit (see page 10)

NOTE

A 1.5cm (⅝in) seam allowance is
used throughout unless otherwise
specified. For a clean, professional
look, finish the raw edges of the
fabric as you work (see page 40),
using your preferred method.

One very effective way to transform a sleeveless garment is to stitch sleeves into the armhole. The choice of fabric and sleeve length are totally in your control, though there are a few things to consider. A fabric that is too heavy could mean that the sleeves end up weighing down the rest of the garment. It's also advisable to go for a fabric of a similar colour to the original, to ensure that the colours do not run into each other in the wash. Follow the steps below to make lightweight 'flutter' sleeves that are perfect for a summer top or dress.

1. Unpick the hem or bias tape finishing around the armhole of the sleeveless dress or top, and press the hem flat.

2. Measure around the armhole and record this figure.

3. Press the first square of fabric for the sleeve and fold it in four (folding twice). Starting from the point at which all the folds meet, measure 30cm (12in) along the top and right-hand side edges and mark with tailor's chalk. Join the marks to form a curve, then cut along the curve.

Project continues overleaf

3

UPCYCLING PROJECTS

4

4. Open up the fabric: you should have a full circle. Draw a smaller circle a little off-centre, towards the bottom edge of the circle. The circumference of the circle should be the same as the measurement you recorded in step 2. Cut out the circle.

5. Repeat steps 3 and 4 with the other square of sleeve fabric, using the small cut-out circle as a template for the second sleeve.

6. Lay the new sleeves over the armholes and pin them in place, right sides together. Sew around the new sleeve, maintaining the original armhole's seam allowance. Finish off the raw edge around the seam allowance and press the seam towards the sleeve.

7. Finish the raw edge around the sleeve hem (see page 40). Fold the hem to the wrong side by 1cm (⅜in). Press, pin and sew the hem in place.

8. Give your new sleeves a good steam press.

Old jeans tote bag

Old and damaged jeans have lots of potential uses: they can be deliberately distressed and ripped, or even cropped to create shorts. But denim has many other options for re-use, and it lends itself particularly well to this sturdy tote bag for everyday errands and shopping. Consider unpicking the back pockets of the jeans to stitch onto the tote bag for an extra detail.

1. Start by cutting off the legs from your jeans, just above the knees, and cut along the outer seams of each trouser leg. Save the inseams on both sides, as the stitching will serve as decorative detailing.

2. Press both fabric pieces and cut out two rectangles measuring 48 x 35.5cm (19 x 14in). (You can make the rectangles larger or smaller if you wish.) Cut two pieces of interfacing the same size and apply to the wrong side of the denim pieces following the manufacturer's instructions. The interfacing will strengthen and add structure to the bag.

3. From the lightweight lining fabric, cut two rectangles the same as the denim pieces. At the bottom left and right corners of these rectangles, cut out a 5cm (2in) square.

4. From what's left of the jeans, cut out two straps measuring 63.5 x 11.5cm (25 x 4½in).

Project continues overleaf

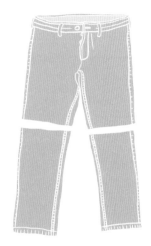

1

5

7

7 – detail

5.   Unpick one of the back pockets from the jeans and pin it to one of the rectangles. Using matching thread and following the original stitch lines, stitch the pocket in place. This will be the front of the bag.

6.   With right sides together, pin the denim rectangles together and sew together around the side and bottom edges, leaving the top edge open. Repeat with the lining fabric, but leave a 13cm (5in) gap in the middle of one side edge.

7.   At the bottom edges of the denim and lining fabrics, pinch the bottom corners so that the side seam is sitting directly over the bottom edge seam, forming a triangle. Pin and sew across the corner. Snip off the corners 1cm (⅜in) from the stitching. Press the seams open.

8.   Fold the straps in half lengthways, with right sides together. Pin and sew along the long unfolded edge. Trim the seam allowances and press the seams open. Using a loop turner, blunt-tipped chopstick or knitting needle, carefully turn the straps right side out.

Project continues overleaf

OLD JEANS TOTE BAG

9. With right sides together, aligning the raw edges and, making sure the straps are not twisted, pin the straps to the top edge of each side of the bag.

10. With right sides together, place the main bag inside the lining, sandwiching the straps in between. Pin and sew around the top edge.

11. Through the gap in the bag lining, pull the tote bag right side out.

12. Fold the raw edges of the lining gap under and edge stitch (see page 35) the opening closed. Topstitch (see page 35) around the top edge of the tote bag and give the bag a final press.

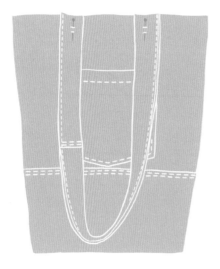

9

10

UPCYCLING PROJECTS

Scrap fabric belt

YOU WILL NEED

Long strips of scrap fabric at least
   15cm (6in) wide
Strip of medium-weight fusible
   (iron-on) interfacing 8cm (3in)
   wide
Two 4.5cm (1½in) D-rings
Basic sewing kit (see page 10)
Blunt-tipped chopstick or
   knitting needle

Instead of throwing away fabric scraps that you accumulate during your upcycling journey, why not turn them into a simple belt? Whether it's styled as a design feature to add character to an outfit, or as an alternative belt option to add a pop of colour to a basic coat, this adjustable fabric belt can elevate any outfit. Select leftovers from mid- to heavyweight fabrics in block colours or with patterns. Woven fabrics such as denim, wax fabrics or mid-weight cotton drill give a relaxed but clean finish. This is also a quick and easy project that you can use to practise using your sewing machine if you are just getting started: you will learn how to sew in straight lines, turn corners and topstitch.

1. Sew your scrap fabric strips together to form one long strip that's twice your waist measurement plus 50cm (20in) in length and 7.5cm (3in) wide. Trim to size if necessary. Press the seams open, then press the whole strip to get rid of any kinks and creases. Fold the strip in half.

2. Cut the strip in two, to give you two pieces each measuring 7.5cm (3in) wide and your waist measurement plus 25cm (10in) in length.

3. Cut a piece of medium-weight interfacing to the same measurement as one of the pieces. Following the manufacturer's instruction, apply the interfacing to the wrong side of one of the pieces.

Project continues overleaf

4. With right sides together, pin the fabrics together and sew around the rectangle with a 1.5-cm (⅝in) seam allowance, leaving an 8cm (3in) gap in one long edge.

5. Trim the corners and turn the belt right side out through the gap. Use an object with a blunt tip, such as a chopstick or a knitting needle, to poke out the corners to make sure the edges are neat and sharp. Give the belt a good steam press.

6. Carefully topstitch (see page 35) all around the belt. This creates a neat, clean finish and also closes the opening.

7. Slide the two D-rings onto one edge of the belt. Fold over roughly 2.5cm (1in) to cover the rings, then sew across the strip as close as possible to the D-rings.

SCRAP FABRIC BELT

Simple headband

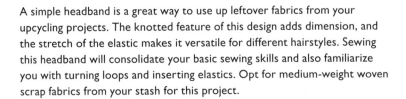

YOU WILL NEED

Two 40.5 x 15cm (16 x 6in) pieces
   of your chosen fabric
One 35.5 x 9cm (14 x 3½in) piece
   of your chosen fabric
15cm (6in) elastic, 2.5cm (1in) wide
Basic sewing kit (see page 10)
Loop turner
Safety pin or bodkin

A simple headband is a great way to use up leftover fabrics from your upcycling projects. The knotted feature of this design adds dimension, and the stretch of the elastic makes it versatile for different hairstyles. Sewing this headband will consolidate your basic sewing skills and also familiarize you with turning loops and inserting elastics. Opt for medium-weight woven scrap fabrics from your stash for this project.

1. Fold each of the two larger fabric pieces in half lengthways, with right sides together. Pin and sew, using a 1.5cm (⅜in) seam allowance. Trim the seam allowance (see page 39) to reduce bulk. Using a loop turner, turn the strips right side out. Repeat with the shorter piece of fabric.

2. Attach a safety pin to one end of the elastic and pass it through the shorter tube, making sure that the elastic does not disappear into the tube. Pin and baste the fabric to the elastic at each end of the tube.

3. Fold one of the larger pieces in half lengthways. Place one end of the elasticated piece on top, matching the raw edges. Fold the excess fabric at the side edges of the larger piece over it and pin all layers together.

3

Project continues overleaf

SIMPLE HEADBAND

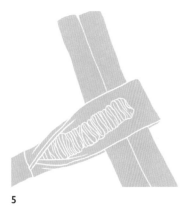

5

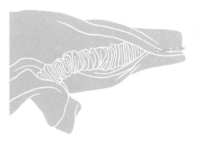

7

4. Sew through all layers. Trim off any stray threads. The larger piece now forms a loop to which the elasticated section is attached.

5. Turn the piece around, so that the stitched elasticated section is on the left. Pass the remaining larger piece through the loop created in the previous step.

6. Repeat steps 3 and 4 with this piece, matching the other end of the elasticated piece to the raw edges of the larger piece and sewing all the layers together.

7. In order to hide the raw ends, pull them through to the right side.

Pockets

I personally would like pockets in every item of clothing in my wardrobe, but I'm aware that they're not everybody's cup of tea! You will notice that most of the sewing patterns in this book do not include pockets in their main instructions, but there is absolutely nothing stopping you adding them on yourself. Adding pockets or improving pockets is also another way to upcycle and add a touch of personality to an existing piece in your wardrobe.

Pockets come in many shapes and forms and can be both functional and decorative. In-seam and patch pockets are the most common and easy-to-sew pockets. In-seam pockets are included in the Josie dress sewing pattern (see page 108), although they are not positioned at the side seams as in most dresses. They are normally inserted within seam lines and have pocket bags hidden on the inside of a garment. Patch pockets, on the other hand, are visible on the garment, and can have straight, angled or curved edges.

PATCH POCKET

Ideally, these pockets should be sewn on when the garment is not fully constructed. For example, if you choose to add patch pockets to the front skirt of the Joy pinafore dress, the pockets should be attached to the skirt front panel before the front and back skirts are fully sewn together. However, if you're adding pockets to improve an existing garment, patch pockets can be sewn on top of already made clothes.

5

7

Tip:
To sew these reinforcing stitches,
use chalk to mark the small triangle
or rectangle to serve as a stitching
guide. Also remember to slow down
your sewing speed and count the
stitches down each side to ensure
both top edges of your pockets look
alike. Backstitch neatly at the start
and finish of the reinforcing stitches.

Straight-edged pocket

1. Trace and cut out the pocket template and cut out the fabric pieces.

2. At the top edge of the pocket, fold 1cm (⅜in) and then a further 2.5cm (1in) to the wrong side and press in place.

3. Carefully unfold the second (larger) fold, then fold it over to the right side of the pocket. Sew down the short sides of the folded section and trim the corners of the seam allowance.

4. Turn the top section through to the wrong side to create a neat, folded edge and press to set the seam.

5. Around the other three edges of the pocket, fold 1.5cm (⅝in) over to the wrong side. Steam press the edges to set them.

6. Pin the pockets in position on the garment and lean the garment against your body. Check the pocket position by looking in the mirror and also slip your hands into the pockets a few times to ensure that the pocket placement works for you. Adjust the pocket position if necessary.

7. When you are happy with the position, edge stitch (see page 35) around the side and bottom edges of the pocket. At the top corners, sew a small triangle or rectangle to reinforce the pocket edge.

Curved pocket

1. Follow steps 1–3 of Straight-edged pocket.

2. Around the curved bottom edge and about two-thirds of the way up the side edges, sew one row of gathering stitches (see page 63) 1cm (⅜in) from the edge.

3. Around the side and bottom edges, fold 1.5cm (⅝in) to the wrong side. At this point, you will notice that the seam allowance around the curve will begin to 'bunch up'. Just gently tug on the loose threads at the end of the gathering stitches to ease the fabric around the curve. Steam-press the edge of the pocket to mould the fabric into shape, then remove the gathering stitches.

4. Attach the pocket to the garment and reinforce the top edges, following steps 6 and 7 of Straight-edged pocket.

Tip:
Cut out a pocket template from card, then mark and cut away the seam allowance. You can then use the template to shape the curved edge of the pocket.

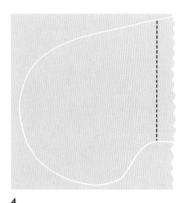

4

In-seam pocket

In-seam pockets commonly feature in dresses, skirts and trousers. They are sewn into the side seams of garment and, if sewn correctly, will be invisible. Note that any sewing patterns for projects in your collection without in-seam pockets can still have in-seam pockets stitched on – just use the in-seam pocket template and follow the steps below. To add in-seam pockets to existing garments, unpick the side seam stitches and apply these same steps.

1. Trace and cut out the in-seam pocket template and use it to cut out two pairs of pocket pieces – a front and back pocket bag for each pocket.

2. Finish the raw edges (see page 40) around the pocket pieces and side seams of your garment.

3. To work out where to position your in-seam pockets, lay the front and back garment pieces flat on a table, right side up. Measure and mark 13cm (5in) down from the waistline.

Tip:
Please note that the 13cm (5in) suggested in step 3 is ideal if the skirt or trousers will sit at or close to your waistline. Certain garments might need this position to be lowered or raised, so drape the fabric against your body to double-check the pocket position. At this point, adjust if necessary and ensure that all the fabric pieces have the mark at the same position.

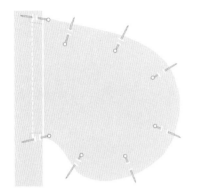

6 – pinning

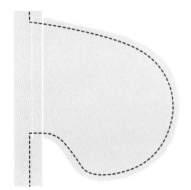

6 – sewing

Tip:
You can use a ruler and chalk to mark out the seam allowance around the side seam and pocket to ensure your pivot points are accurate.

4. With right sides together, aligning the raw edges, place the top edge of the pocket at the marked position on the front of the garment and pin it in place. Sew the pocket to the side seam at a 12mm (½in) seam allowance. Repeat on the back of the garment.

5. Press the pocket bag away from the garment.

6. Place the front and back garment pieces right sides together, aligning the pocket bags. Pin all around the pocket bags and side seams. With a 1.5cm (⅝in) seam allowance, sew along the side seam, stopping and pivoting at the top and bottom of the pocket bags; do not sew all the way down the side seam or you will end up with a closed pocket!

7. Press the garment seams open and press the pocket towards the front of the garment. Double check that the stitches initially used to attach the pocket bags are hidden.

Index

Acknowledgements

I always wondered what writing a book would be like and I have many people to thank for making the experience a great and inspiring learning curve. From my loving husband, Ken to my not-so-little daughter, Olivia and to my entire family for their support. I have huge thanks to Lori, Simone and Florida, my amazing friends, for the much-appreciated check-ins and emotional support they gave me throughout the journey.

To the entire team at Octopus Publishing, especially Ellie Corbett, my amazing editor whose support helped me get through the ups and downs of sewing, photographing the sewing process and writing the sewing instructions. It truly has been an inspiring experience and the beginning of greater things to come.

About the author

Juliet Uzor is a London-based mum and school teacher with a huge love of sewing clothes. In a bid to own a wardrobe full of clothes that fit her body and represent her love of colour, patterns and different textures, she taught herself to sew her own clothes in 2013. That love and dedication led to her winning the *Great British Sewing Bee* in 2019. In order to inspire other home sewers, encourage crafting for good mental health and demystify the sewing of clothes, she enjoys sharing fun sewing and DIY craft videos on her YouTube channel and other social media pages.

Scan here to download the patterns for all of the projects.